The Philosophy of Liberation

The Philosophy of Liberation

Revisiting Genuine Religious Experiences with Special Reference to Christianity

By
Cyril Desbruslais SJ

Edited by
Kuruvilla Pandikattu SJ

Christian World Imprints™

&

Jnana-Deepa Vidyapeeth

First Published in 2016 by

Christian World Imprints™
Christian Publishing & Books from India
H-12 Bali Nagar, **New Delhi-110015**
info@christianworldimprints.com
www.ChristianWorldImprints.com
Phone: +91 11 25465925

&

Jnana-Deepa Vidyapeeth
Ramwadi, Nagar Road, **Pune-411014**
jdvoffice@jdv.edu.in
www.jdv.edu.in
Phone: +91 20 41036111

ISBN: 978-93-5148-129-4 (HB) ISBN: 978-93-5148-130-0 (PB)

This text book is a part of Jnana-Deepa Vidyapeeth's attempt to provide resource materials for self-study and distance education.

Printed at D. K. Fine Art Press Pvt. Ltd.

Dedicated to the Staff and Students of
Jnana-Deepa Vidyapeeth, Pune, my beloved
Alma Mater where I spent 8 memorable
years as a student of Philosophy and then
of Theology and later spent 37 meaningful
years as a Philosophy Faculty staff.

THE BOOK

The author assumes that Theology of Liberation is a completely new hermeneutics, which involves re-thinking of the entire Christian experience from the perspective of the oppressed. However, for all its richness and promise, Theology of Liberation is, to a great extent, irrelevant for Asia in general and for India in particular. This is because the starting point of Theology of Liberation is the Scriptures of a tiny minority religion, which would not be able to motivate the vast majority of the people in India and Asia.

So, this book is a philosophical look at liberation and how we can free ourselves based on well-tested guidelines. The book is a radical, critical attempt at evolving a Philosophy of Liberation for Asia. It tries to build up a down-to-earth and critico-reflective vision of reality, founded on the human person in his/her entirety, that would sensitise us to oppressive and liberative understandings of man, woman, God and the world.

THE AUTHOR

Cyril Desbruslais SJ (born 21 December 1940 at Calcutta) is an Indian Jesuit priest, Associate Professor of Philosophy at Jnana-Deepa Vidyapeeth, Pune and an accomplished playwright. He has taught various courses like "Philosophical Anthropology," "Philosophy of God," "Rites and Rituals," "History of Western Philosophy" and "Philosophy of Liberation" in his more than forty years of teaching career. He has been writing and directing every year a creative play which has relevant social themes for more than 25 years.

EDITOR'S PREFACE

Dr. Cyril Desbruslais SJ, is an effective counsellor, committed teacher and a successful playwright. I am delighted to introduce him and his works, especially since he is celebrating 75 glorious years of his life this year.

As a counsellor, he would accompany, both the young and old, and inspire them. He started the group "Searching in Service and Unity" in 1971, when he was beginning his Theology studies at De Nobili College, Pune, India. Based on his personal experience, he wanted to give a home to the youth who are seeking. He wanted to set up an inter-denominational youth group, one made up of young people of different religious and ethnic backgrounds. He wanted to celebrate our differences, not just sweep them under the carpet and so reached out to people of various identities. By these common activities, he helped the youth to develop a deep social sense, a sense of responsibility and concern for the poor, the deprived and all victims of injustice, in our country and all over the world – and do something creative about it.

As a philosopher, he has contributed significantly to Jnana-Deepa Vidyapeeth, Pune. In an interview given to *DNC Times*, he put it succinctly: "I suppose it's to help all people become more fully human, more fully alive. That would also imply recognizing that beauty is unity in diversity. Unity without diversity is uniformity, and that's boring; diversity without beauty is jarring and garish, and that's ugly. We, the so-called clergy, must be prepared to do a little more listening and learning and a good deal of less talking and teaching. Each of us, can learn how to better and appreciate our faith and culture by being more open to, and learning from, the views of others.

He was exposed to liberation theology during his Theology studies (1971–1974) at JDV and was deeply moved by it. As Gustavo Gutiérrez had put it, liberation theology is not a mere re-hashing of the old doctrinal theses with a new emphases. It is oppressed people ("under the boot") who are enunciating a theology, from their oppressed perspective. And that is a totally new way of looking at things. And wasn't the Bible addressed primarily to them? But, one might ask, "Could such uneducated, illiterate and dehumanised people theologise/philosophise at all?" Yes, affirms Paulo Freire. No matter how brain-washed into considering themselves as unimportant, brutish and ignorant such people were - for however many centuries - they *were* still capable (with a little help) to critique their situation, to give new definitions ("names") to reality and initiate startlingly new praxis (action-plans as the fruit of critico-reflection).

General Congregation XXXII of the Society of Jesus put it more forcefully when it spoke of the "inseparable link" between faith formation and building up God's kingdom (action for justice). And then there was Fr. Pedro Arrupe SJ, the man who helped put the Society of Jesus back on its radical path again. He was convinced that this was the way to live out the Christian, Jesuit way of life in today's world.

But, it suddenly dawned on him that liberation theology, however fine and noble and biblical an endeavour it may be, was irrelevant to Asia in general and India in particular, precisely because it was a Biblical endeavor. What we need is united action for justice and liberation by *all* Indians, inspired with a common vision. And this common vision could *not* be the Holy Book of one religion, but a shared understanding of the human person.

Yet, it seemed to him that we must, through dialogue, establish some sort of common base for this or we'd have no grounds for praise or blame, there'd be no real criterion to challenge white supremacism or the caste system. So, he dialogued with people (common people, youth of all religions and their families, from his youth group, and all over the country and abroad, not forgetting to talk over controversial issues with academics and University professors, too) and eventually formulated an understanding of "common human nature, adequately understood."

The content of his reflections, carried on at a critical academic level, were tested in his work among youth and older people of all religions and further tested by action-reflection in his work among quarry-workers, street children, prostitutes and their offspring, slum-dwellers, etc. Like Plato and some existential thinkers, he presented a more popular form of his liberation philosophy in over 20 plays, written by him and enacted by youngsters of all creeds and communities for over 40 years, mainly in Pune.

Out of these numerous committed engagement came out "Philosophy of Liberation," his favourite course. It may be noted that he has given more than ten different courses at Jnana-Deepa Vidyapeeth, all of which were highly appreciated. We are happy to present these reflections to the public with the hope that it will benefit many more people of goodwill.

Personally, I am happy to have attended and profited enormously from his course about thirty years ago, which I still cherish. So, bringing out this work is part of gratitude towards him. Unhesitatingly, I would recommend this book to those interested in deepening their religious convictions and experiencing the depth of reality, which will truly liberate us!

Dr. Kuruvilla Pandikattu SJ
Dean of Philosophy
Faculty of Philosophy
Jnana-Deepa Vidyapeeth
Pune 411015

December 21, 2015
Desbruslais' 75th birthday

(The material for this preface is adapted from the Wikipedia entry on Cyril Desbruslais)

ACKNOWLEDGEMENT

Philosophy of Liberation was always my favourite subject. I could not have written it without the support of my students. For the first few years I had no notes, just kept bouncing my ideas of them and learning from their reactions, comments and questions. Some of my most "original" ideas and insights were inspired by them.

I am also extremely indebted to two fine priests and true gentlemen: **Frs Jean de Marneffe SJ** and **Aloysius Schlegel SJ**. The former, more than anyone else, initiated me into the Groves of Academe, as also sowed in me the seeds of a deep love for philosophy, The latter, a librarian par excellence, helped me in the references and bibliography for this and all the other courses I taught at JDV. Without him and the splendid library he built up, I would never have been able to teach or write anything worthwhile.

CONTENTS

INTRODUCTION

"O Liberty what crimes are committed in thy name!"

-Mme Roland on the way to the guillotine

The Theology of Liberation

We are all familiar with "The Theology of Liberation." In fact, it has become so well known that even the most repressive of systems have tried to hijack its terminology and exploit it to publicise and justify some of their worst atrocities. There are even those who are so used to its vocabulary that they will decry it as out dated, *passé* – as if ideas are to be snapped up and discarded solely because of their novelty or age and not because they are relevant, challenging or insightful!

We need to be reminded, however, that the Theology of Liberation is no mere re-hashing of traditional theses and dogmas, such that their implications become explicitly clearer in the field of Hope or Politics ("Theology of Hope",[1] "Theology of Politics"[2]). Unlike such approaches, however praiseworthy they may be in themselves, liberation theology is a completely new hermeneutic it involves a re-thinking of the entire Christian experience from the perspective of

1 Jürgen Moltmann. 1993. *Theology of Hope: On the Ground and the Implications of a Christian Eschatology*. 1st ed. Minneapolis: Fortress Press.

2 Micklem, Nathaniel. 1941. *The Theology of Politics*. London, New York etc.: Oxford University Press.

the oppressed or, as Gustavo Gutiérrez – one of its founding fathers put it – it is "theologizing from the underside of the boot."[3]

All previous theologizing had been from the other end, from the point of view of the one wearing the boot! Not that Karl Rahner and Edward Schillebeeckx or even Thomas Aquinas and Augustine of Hippo, were insensitive oppressors of the poor, who were deliberately grinding them into the mire under their cruel boots. Far from it: many of these committed Christian thinkers did their level best to see things from the perspective of the *Anawim Jahwe* (the little ones' of the Lord). But even if they often did succeed in being an effective voice for the voiceless and startling the rest of us from our bourgeois slumber, still they had not known and experienced first-hand what the wretched of the earth have had to undergo for centuries. They did not grow up in an atmosphere or uncertainty or terror. They never saw their children die in convulsions, carried off by a disease that could have been staved off for the price of one person's dinner in a Five-Star Hotel. They never had to face eons of insult and deprivation, never had to watch helplessly while their mothers sisters and daughters were raped, their children sexually abused and their land ravaged. However much they might have felt *for* them, they hardly had to feel *with* them the hopelessness and helplessness that was their lot. Liberation Theology is theology enunciated by these impoverished people, often illiterate, who had been made to believe that they were uncultured, at best, little better than beasts of burden.

The God of the most well-intentioned First-World Christian is very different from the God of the Dalit. Whether you theologise in the relative comfort of a religious house or an academic institution in the temperate Occident ... or with an empty belly, under the blazing sun and the nauseous smell of the Third-World slum – all this will have a major impact on how you read the Gospels, pray, celebrate ... and see God.

It is indeed remarkable how the reflections and sharings of such illiterate (or merely marginally educated) peasants and slum-dwellers

3 Gustavo Gutiérrez. 1988. *A Theology of Liberation: History, Politics, and Salvation*. Maryknoll, N.Y.: Orbis Books. See also Gutiérrez, Gustavo; Marc H. Ellis and Otto Maduro. 1989. *The Future of Liberation Theology: Essays in Honor of Gustavo Gutiérrez*. Maryknoll, N.Y.: Orbis Books.

can add insightful perspectives to the learned commentaries of PhDs and polyglot scholars. Ernesto Cardenal's Three-Volume *Gospel in Solentiname* is an excellent case in point.[4] Solentiname is the rough name given to an area comprising some thirty-eight islands in Nicaragua. On the largest of these is a Basic Christian Community, founded by the priest-poet who is the editor and publisher of the trilogy. Here, we read a faithful record of the sharing of the simple people on the Sunday readings at Mass. Cardinal introduces his "theologians" to us:

> Marcelino is a mystic. Olivia is more often theological. Rebecca, Marcelino's wife, always stresses love. Iaureano refers everything to the revolution. Elvis always thinks of the perfect society of the future. Felipe, another young man, very conscious of the proletarian struggle. Old Tomas Pella, his father, doesn't know how to read, but he talks with great wisdom. Alejandro, Olivia's son, is a young leader, and his commentaries are usually directed toward everyone, and especially toward other young people. Pancho is a conservative. Julio Mairena is a great defender of equality. His brother Oscar always talks about unity . . .

And here, on the opening pages of Volume I, is the fruit of their shared reflections on the first chapter of John's Gospel.

Manuel read the Prologue aloud. Then we commented on each verses:

> In the beginning was the Word,
> and the Word was with God,
> and the Word was God.

There was a long silence. Afterwards Felipe spoke: "Christ brought a message from God that was very important for the people, and that meant that He was the Word. But it wasn't just any word. It was a serious word, which didn't deceive. He is the word of God

4 Ernesto Cardenal. 1976. *Gospel in Solentiname,* New York: Orbis Books in an excellent translation by Donald D. Walsh.

and so He's a true word. And this word came into the word, and has remained among us."

Alejandro: "I think that when they call Christ the Word it's because God expresses Himself through him. He expresses Himself to denounce oppression, to say: 'Here there is injustice, here there is evil, there are rich and poor, the earth belongs to a few.' And to announce a new life, a new truth, in a word: a social change. With that word God frees us...."

The Philosophy of Liberation

All this is very interesting, very inspiring and very challenging. But, for all its richness and promise, the Theology of Liberation is, to a great extent, irrelevant for Asia in general and for India in particular. Why? Since its starting point is the Scriptures of a tiny minority religion and would not be able to motivate the vast majority of the people, The Theology of Liberation would be accessible, at best, to a mere 2.5% of India's teeming millions (and let us not forget that a sizable proportion of that little flock – including a good number of the clergy and perhaps more than half the hierarchy) would be decidedly not in sympathy with it at all, would probably denounce it as Marxist, "mere politics disguised as religion" and a diabolical attempt to subvert the established order of religion and society. What about the over 97% of our fellow-citizens who would not resonate with the Bible? Even if there are some non-Christians who, like Gandhiji, professed admiration for the Sermon on the Mount (and he apparently recognised its radical, social message far better than most Indian Christians), would they not – as the Father of the Nation once admitted – turn, for strength and reassurance, in times of depression and discouragement, not to the words of Jesus but, more spontaneously to the Gita? And isn't this natural? In "limit experiences" we seek inspiration from our religious roots. Would not each of the priests who are members of our Indian Studies Department turn rather to the New Testament in a moment of crisis? Though with their knowledge of Sanskrit and Indology, they have frequently been touched by passages in the epics, the Koran or the Dhammapada? Should we then encourage each community to develop its own Theology of Liberation from its respective Scriptures?

But this would divide us all the more. Is there no hope for a common platform of committed action to all Indians of goodwill who want to do something to liberate our land and people?

India is a religious country. But Indian religiosity is often more of a blessing in disguise. True, God has been sought in our land with a relentless desire ever since time began. True, India has been the cradle of many of the world's great religions and this land has welcomed many foreign faiths, letting them take deep root in her soil when they were being hounded, persecuted and proscribed in many another "civilised" nation. But it is also incontestably true that religions in India, especially nowadays – as developed by clerical, political and other vested interests-have perpetuated all manner of superstition, obscurantism, irrationalism and oppression. Indeed, they have often given a questionable religious basis to unjust and dehumanising social structures that have resulted in the oppression of women, the subjugation of the majority by a privileged minority and facilitated the accumulation of wealth, power and land by a few advantaged families or ethnic groups. Priestcraft has been the bane of religion in our land, as elsewhere in the world. Indeed, it can arguably be maintained that no single group of men (the choice of the masculine word is deliberate) has, down the ages, so effectively oppressed people as priests-the whole tribe of them, from witch-doctors and shamans, the various "priestly" tribes, right down to the reverend fathers and pastors of Christianity. Nietzsche inveighed against Christianity as "the immortal blemish of mankind" inasmuch as it taught its adepts to hate the world, to be suspicious of all that is human or even embodied, to embrace all that is ugly, unhappy and sad. However, we may protest against this "unfair generalisation" and cry out that it is but a "miserable caricature" of Christianity that he is ridiculing, we can't deny that this caricature is the more common currency in use than the genuine article ... and little effort is being made to remedy this malady! Do not Nietzsche's fulminations apply with at least equal relevance to other Indian religions as well? Many a stout-hearted Hindu reformer – as also the much-maligned Ashgar Ali Engineer among his Islamic correligionists – has come to grief, trying to weed out the cockle from the good wheat of authentic religion.

What we need in India today-as well as in Asia, and-why not? – in today's world at large – is a radical, critical Philosophy of Liberation. We need to build up a down-to-earth and critico-reflective vision of reality, founded on the human person in his/her entirety, that would sensitise us to oppressive and liberative understandings of man, woman, God, the world, and so on. As we shall see, even notions like Freedom and Justice are susceptible to an oppressive interpretation. Nor should we let ourselves be deterred in our task by the charge that these are mere concepts – "words, words, words" as Hamlet would say. Far from being mere academic conceptual bickering that have naught to do with the raw business of life, let alone the struggle for Justice, these key concepts have a direct bearing on how we view, and respond to, the existential situation. As Chesterton once put it so well, "Nothing is more practical than a good theory."[5] Nothing determines our actions more profoundly than our basic notions. Such presuppositions influence how we dream or plan, how we act and to what extent we will be committed to the struggle for justice.

For instance, take the idea of freedom. When we come across a person who assures us that he is "all for freedom," our natural tendency is to congratulate ourselves on having found a staunch ally in the struggle for human liberation. But, very often, such a person is no more than a rank capitalist whose sole goal is the establishment of a "free" market that will enable him to have unbridled sway over prices, supply and production curves-the very things that would further oppress and dehumanize the people we would be seeking to liberate. Freedom could be understood as "the right to have more" (be it at the expense of some others) or "the right to be more" for everyone (even if this would involve putting a curb on the capacities of some to accumulate, amass and hoard).

The basis, or better, the criterion of a liberative understanding of reality-as far as the Philosophy of Liberation is concerned-is the human person, taken in his or her entirety. A liberative understanding of the human person is one that would promote the overall growth

5 The saying is also attributed to the psychologist Kurt Lewin. 1951. *Field Theory in Social Science; Selected Theoretical Papers.* 1st ed. New York: Harper. p. 169. Sometimes it is also attributed to Albert Einstein.

and development of the entire human composite in a balanced and harmonious way, as well as one that seeks the well-being of all humans, without ruthlessly sacrificing the development of those of a particular sex, colour or social/geographical grouping in order that some favoured section may better its prospects. To use a well-worn phrase, an authentic philosophy of liberation envisages the building up of authentic persons who are "fully human, fully alive."

The problem is that the human person is a rich, multi-faceted, myriad-minded dynamic whole. It is all too easy to seek the fulfillment of one aspect of him/her to the detriment of others. Indeed, it is not even possible to seek the fulfillment of every human longing with equal intensity. For example, an unbridled attempt to indulge one's appetite for food and drink might bring one joy and pleasure for some time but would eventually ruin the health of the entire person. If I feel a stirring of my loins when a particularly delectable (and helpless) woman crosses my path and, with reckless abandon, set about fulfilling my sexual urge at her expense ... wouldn't this frustrate my overall growth as a human being? As we shall see, rape doesn't only dehumanise the victim: it animalises the very aggressor! In other words, before we can go one step further, we should try to seek out a balanced, harmonious, (w) holistic – in a word liberative! – understanding of the human person.

But can we do this? How do we know that our allegedly liberative understanding is not – maybe even unconsciously – a disguised, one-sided and oppressive one, after all? Well, we can at least try to do so. Above all, in dialogue with sincere people of other approaches we can become aware of such possible biases and come closer to such a goal. As we shall see, one's overall philosophical vision, if it is to remain open to liberation, can never be a closed ideological stance, a once-and-for-all static system, but a tentative framework, one that is ever open to challenge and, if necessary, adaptation or change.

A Voice from the Anawim

"To me, one's destiny is controlled by a mysterious hand that moves all things. Only for the select do things turn out as planned; to those of us who are born to be tamale-eaters, heaven sends only tamales. We plan and plan and some little thing happens to wash it all away."

Like once, I decided to save and I said to (my wife) Paula, 'Old girl, put away this money so that we'll have a little pile.' When we had ninety pesos laid away, pum! my father got sick and I had to give all to him for doctors and medicines. It was the only time I tried to save. I said to Paula, 'There you are. Why should we try to save if someone gets sick and we have to spend it all?' Sometimes I even think that saving brings on illness! That's why I firmly believe that some of us are born to be poor and remain that way no matter how hard we struggle and pull this way and that. God gives us just enough to go vegetating, no?[6]

The Voice of the Church

Never before today has man been so keenly aware of freedom, yet at the same time, new forms of social and psychological slavery make their appearance.[7]

6 Manuel, in Oscar Lewis. 1961. *The Children of the Son*. New York: Random House, p. 171.

7 *Documents of Vatican II*, "Church in the Modern World," No. 4.

Chapter 1

THE HUMAN PERSON CRITERION OF LIBERATION

Introduction

What does it mean to be human? This is the crucial question that we have to deal with now for on our response will depend our whole approach to the philosophy of liberation. Of course, we mustn't be so naive as to imagine that we can adequately define the human person, neatly set limits to what we are and what we are not. As Gabriel Marcel rightly points out, what we are busying ourselves with now is a "mystery-question" and not a "problem". In simple language, we are asking ourselves a question of which we are a part. Hence, we cannot detach ourselves from it, view it objectively and scientifically and thence work out an exhaustive, final, once-and-for-all answer- as would be the case if we were dealing with a problem. Thus, the best we can hope for in a situation like this is to throw more light on the issue and that's all. Seeking a response to a mystery is like taking one more step towards an ever-receding horizon. After all, a mystery is not merely "something that goes over our heads" (which is the traditional theological understanding of the term). Rather it is something that is so rich in meaning that, try as we might, for as long as we can, we will never be able to fully exhaust all its meaning.

This is most evident in the case of love and friendship: no matter how many years we love somebody, no matter how long we live together in close companionship, we discover more and more about that person every day. That's why true love, true friendship, never gets boring: we can't get to know a person inside-out and through and through. Some shallow people may think that they do, but they are wrong-grossly and foolishly wrong. We might be able to come up with strict definitions in the positive sciences (let the scientists tell us these) but, in the sphere of mystery, all we expect is a helpful pointer: only that and nothing more.

The Facts

Before we look at the concrete human condition of people all over the earth, we begin with a more general, long-distance view. After this, we shall begin to zoom in onto the more existential situation.

When we, the human reality, look around us at the world we live in, we notice three types of beings, basically. In the first category, there is what has been traditionally called the "mineral kingdom". This comprises a vast and multifarious array of elements and compounds, some solid, some liquid and some gaseous. These are "inorganic" or "non-living things"(we shall seek out a "pointer definition" of life is a moment). Then there is the "vegetable kingdom", wherein we enter the realm of "living things". Under this rubric we find another innumerable host: plants, trees, flowers, vegetables, fruit and the like: all these undergo change, grow and die. Finally, there is the "animal kingdom", consisting of living beings that, unlike plants, are able to move and have highly developed sensations. The multitude of reptiles, birds, insects, fish, as well as "animals proper", together with their varieties of species and sub-species make up this grouping.

What We Have in Common with Other Things

Let's begin with the mineral kingdom. What do we have in common with it? Well, to begin with, our" body is 65% oxygen, 18% carbon, about 11.5 % calcium, 1% phosphorus and 1.5% other elements. In other words, there is in us no element (or compound for that matter: we are, for example, 70% water) that is not found in nature. The world around us and ourselves is made up of the same basic ingredients! There is a kind of literalness in the words of poets and mystics who claim that "We are cousins of the stone's and our sisters are the stars". And have we not been told by a doctor, for instance, that we need some more iron in our diet (though, of course, it wouldn't quite work if we tried to eat a nail!) Truly, we are of the planet earth.

As for the vegetable kingdom, it is characterised by four basic "living activities": growth, reproduction, nourishment and repair. And we share, together with all members of this kingdom, these activities. We too grow to maturity, take in food, produce offspring, repair injuries and wounds (unless they are very severe ones!) and, like plants, we grow old and die. In short, the vegetable kingdom shares with us the same chemical composition and activities.

Finally, there is the animal kingdom, which, in addition to the four basic vegetative activities outlined above, is also capable-in various degrees-of two more. The first is locomotion (the ability to move oneself). Animals get up and go in search of food: they are not rooted to one place, like a plant. Besides, they give clear evidence of sensation: they can see, hear, smell and respond to touch (often at a higher level of sensitivity than we humans). They can feel pain and pleasure, too. All these animal activities we share. Heedless to say, animals are capable of all vegetative activities and are made up of the same elements and compounds we find in the mineral kingdom.

Thus, there is a lot that we are, have, and do, in common with observable reality, with all that apparently encircles us.

What Is "Life"?

The time has come to ask ourselves what we mean when we say that a thing has life, is alive. If we reflect a bit, we will realise that "life" is a kind of short-hand term for a whole complex of activities and, when a being gives evidence of them, we say that it is "alive". Is there some trait that runs through this whole "complex of activities"? Well, in everyday life, we often say something like, "Look: it's moving! It must be alive!" In other words, we spontaneously and naturally identify life with movement. And, when we say "movement", of course we mean "self-movement": after all, a car or a computer "moves", but they require someone to turn on the ignition and drive, or turn them on and start tapping at keys. A being which moves without any outside interference would be what we call "alive": life is self-movement. Here, of course, we are taking movement in a broader sense than mere transposition from one place to another. We are including under "movement" the very general meaning of "change". Indeed, the Latin root-word *moveri* means change in general (which comprises also change of place). So, in this sense, growth, nourishment, reproduction and repair (all vegetative activities) would be examples of movement.

But is this sufficient as a good working definition of life? In the light of contemporary scientific development, perhaps a further refinement would be necessary. We know today that there is tremendous activity in the sub-atomic world: sub-atomic particles whirl around at break-neck speed round some central core. Would we be prepared to say that sub-atomic particles-neutrons, protons, electrons and so on-are alive? They assuredly are in motion and seem to be moving themselves. And what of the planets? We notice, however, a key difference between this type of "movement" and that of the most elementary forms of plant "life". The former activity merely maintains the status quo: the proton or electron, for all its hectic activity, remains a proton or electron. It doesn't grow, nourish itself, reproduce or repair its "wounds": it cannot. Vegetative activity (the lowest form of "life") is self–perfective. Hence, for practical purposes-as is borne out by phenomenology-we should say that life is self-perfective activity.

In What Way Humans Are Unique?

However, close attention to the facts also assures us that there are certain activities that we humans elicit which distinguish us from the non-human world: only *we* are capable of these. I wish to single out three such: conceptual language, creativity and religion. Perhaps the list could be prolonged. I prefer to limit myself to these three. They are sufficient for my purpose and, at the same time, are fairly evident to everyone. Let us look at each of these in turn.

Conceptual language: Please note, I am not saying that only humans have a language, a means of communication. Even ants have some kind of language. When one of them discovers some grains of sugar on the ground, it goes off and summons others to help carry them away (maybe tapping its feelers on the ground, as the entomologists tell us). But animal communication is confined to the here and now, to the immediately sensible. But we humans can, by means of abstract ideas and concepts, exchange theories and notions that' soar far beyond what is here and now visible and audible.

Creativity: Humans are forever coming up with new styles of architecture, dress and art. Cultures vary in every detail, from language to cuisine. Animals do have some kind of instinctive know-how: how to construct their burrows or nests, how to procure their food and such like. Some have a more or less elaborate "mating dance". But these remain fixed: there is a total lack of creative or artistic variation. Crows all over the world make the same raucous noise, seek out the same food and build the same type of nest. The only "innovation" that some animals (like apes) have been able to come out with is a slight modification of a given observable set up (as when a chimpanzee learned that re-arranging packing cases on the ground would enable it to reach a bunch of bananas overhead).

Religion: We humans are the only beings in the observable world who have been able to form some sort of an understanding of the deity. Only we have elaborated religions which concern the whole area of human existence. Various rites and rituals, various beliefs and doctrines about, say the afterlife, have existed among humans since the dawn of recorded history. There is nothing comparable to this that has ever been observed among animals.

Transcendence

The common note in each of these three uniquely human activities is the fact that they evince a capacity to go beyond the limitations of immediate sense data. Only we have the ability to go beyond the immediately accessible, to transcend. It is in this sense that the German theologian Wolfhart Pannenberg remarks that only humans have a world; animals, at best, have an environment. Only humans can raise questions about what lies over the next hill. Only humans can form a notion of Pune, India, Asia, the World... The "world" of an animal is its immediate environment. Thus, Pannenberg defined the human person by inventing a long German word, *Weltoffenheit* (literally, world-open-ness). I will have occasion to explain later why I think this is, all the same, too passive a definition of the dynamic reality that we are. The human person is not merely passively "open" to the world. In us there is a powerful drive within that pushes us to the world without. We are driven towards the world!

Reflections

A very natural question that could arise in us at this point is, how is it that only humans can transcend their environment? Why is it that even the most developed animals can't go beyond the immediate data of the senses? It seems to me that there are two ways of answering this haunting question. One is to postulate that there is in us a special ingredient that is totally absent in the make-up of the sub-human world and that is what enables us to do what the latter cannot. The other is to suggest that the reason why we can do what the others can't is not because we have something unique that they don't have, but that the same constituents are found in both: the only difference is that in humans, by a process of evolution, these constituents have been able to refine themselves to such an extent that they have become capable of transcendence. In the sub-human world, where these constituents are more or less fixated at a less developed level, transcendence remains impossible.

The more traditional approach-certainly the one favoured by most religious thinkers – is the former. We humans are capable of transcendence because we, and we alone, have a "spiritual soul". The sub-human world has not and that is why we can do what they can't. The term "soul" is, of course, as old as Plato, but Thomistic Christian thought doesn't invest it with the same connotations as the ancient Greeks did. For them, the body-soul relationship was a totally negative one (the former component, the body, was conceived as a kind of prison-cell for the soul, in which it had been immured as punishment for some primeval and obscure fault) and the two were ever at loggerheads with each other in as malefic a manner as one could ever imagine. The human person was basically a soul, plain and simple. The body was as external as the shirt one wears (or the walls of one's prison). This dichotomous conception of the human person is not without advantages, however. For one thing, it provides a simple "proof" for life after death: when we die it is only the material, composite body that decomposes or falls apart into its constituent parts. The "soul", because it is spiritual (i.e. having no parts) is thereby naturally immortal and can go marching on, while the body is a-mouldering in the grave. All living things-including plants and animals-have souls, too (the soul being defined as the *principium vitale* or life source), but these are merely immaterial and not spiritual (they are "intrinsically dependent" on matter and so cannot survive when the latter crumbles). A further possible positive side-effect of this approach is that it affords us a convenient way of showing our superiority to "the other things of this world": we alone have this superior element and this accounts for our superior, actions and status.

But there is the "less orthodox" interpretation of the same facts-the kind of one championed by Teilhard de Chardin SJ and others. According to this understanding, humans can transcend because the matter in us has reached a higher level of complexity, through evolution, than that in animals, plants and the mineral order. Consciousness and the ability to transcend arise when matter has attained a certain "threshold of complexity". Hence, what distinguishes us from the "lower levels" of being is not some special ingredient but the same ingredients in a higher level of complexity. This way of looking at things labours under the grave disadvantage-for some people-of closing the door to any possible rational argument for life after death. All that one is left with is a faith conviction that the grave is not the end of the road. Thus, Teilhard most certainly upheld the Christian doctrine of the resurrection of the entire human person after death, but based his assurance of this on biblical revelation, something that could not be rationally demonstrated (at least, not with cogent, conclusive syllogistic argumentation). On the positive side, it proffers a far more integrated and holistic vision of the human person than the more common Thomistic theory. For, granted that the human person is not seen by neo-Thomists in such a negative and dichotomised manner as in the Platonic view, it still results in a somewhat attenuated unity in the composite (with plenty of crypto-prejudices against the body implied). Teilhard's vision, on the other hand, emphasises our oneness with the rest of reality, a positive point for all who, like him, have-or wish to have-a sense of love and mystical feeling of oneness for the "earth".

Which of the two possible interpretations of the human person should one adopt? Both are equally valid from a hermeneutical point of view (inasmuch as both explain all the facts, without distortion or exaggeration). I think it's basically a question of which interpretation implicitly affirms better those values which are paramount to one's *Weltanschauung* or overall world-view. And it seems to me that Teilhard's point of view is more liberative. It doesn't glorify "spirit" as against its alleged contrary (if not contradictory), matter, nor unduly set off the human person over and against "the world" (from which it would only be a short step to characterise the latter as "dangerous", an "occasion of sin" or even a "vale of tears"). The Thomistic doctrine is surely more liberative than that of Plato but not as liberative as that of Teilhard. What we need is a perspective of the human person in which the tendency to sacrifice (if not ignore) the "material" for the "spiritual" is at least minimal, if not excluded altogether.

What I am getting at will become clearer, perhaps, if I try to illustrate my assertion by reference to some concrete, examples from the history of human thought. Actually, the more common and traditional view has quite an elite crew in its support. This would include most Christian thinkers, quite a few canonised Catholic saints and not a few Indian sages from the classical and contemporary periods.

Plato-Augustine: It is a regrettable fact that St. Augustine, the first influential Christian thinker, who left his mark on many early dogmatic formulations, should have been so influenced by a man who had such a negative attitude to the human body. It would seem that much of the saintly bishop's thinking about "original sin" and. "the Fall" had more to do with Plato than the Genesis story. It is from that earlier source, rather than the Gospels, that we can derive that spirituality that would urge us to "love the things of heaven and despise the things of earth", as the old Post-Communion Prayer of the feast of the Sacred Heart would put it. Thence flows all the distrust of the body and the wicked world, the excesses of the Stylites and flagellants ... as well as the suspicion of emotions, feelings, anything non-rational. In the aftermath of Vatican II a lot of "Christian spirituality" had to be unlearned by many of us. As Samuel Rayan once put it, "Traditional Christian thought is more faithful to Aristotle and Plato than the Bible". Paul Ricoeur is even more blunt: in his view most Christian spirituality is mere "Platonism adapted for mass consumption". All this involves a very oppressive understanding of the human person, where the' body-element is looked down upon, despised and abused and the spirit-soul is seen as all-noble, all-holy and all-pure. No wonder Christians formerly neglected their responsibilities for this world, for human justice and the building up of God's kingdom. As Nikolai Berdyaev wrote, "Marxism bears witness to a forgotten task of Christianity".

Aristotle-Thomas: According to this combine, "body" and "soul" are not to be conceived of as two complete beings in perpetual conflict with each other (as Plato and Company did), but as two principles of being, complementing each other. More precisely, the human person is not seen by this school as a union of body and soul but of prime matter informed by the human soul, its substantial form. Hence arises the traditional Thomistic definition of the human person as *animal rationale* or rational animal.

This seems to be, at first sight, an excellent definition, by way of genus (animal) and specific difference (rational). We are generically animals but our capacity to reason is what raises us above them. This is a more balanced view. The body is not viewed askance, but is assigned a more positive role in human life and activity. But is it really so liberative as it appears?

Karl Marx: When Marx summed up the human person as a "worker" he was, in effect, underscoring in an even more vivid manner our essential oneness. For Marx, we are not human so much when we stop short at reasoning, but when we incarnate that rational envisaging into some creative expression (or work!). The truly human person, for Marx, is not the armchair philosopher, busily ratiocinating in solitary isolation, but the worker who applies his rational capacity to realise some concrete project. Of course we can't deny that Marx erred by over-stressing (in reaction) the other side of the coin. He disregarded anything that seemed particularly mental or "spiritual": he overvalued manual work and tended to downgrade artistic or organisational endeavour. In fact, he had no time for any supra-material human needs. For him, we are basically economic animals, needing food, clothing and shelter-little else. He doesn't devote much space to human transcendence and the needs it generates.

Karl Rahner: One of the greatest thinkers of our time, the German Jesuit and theologian, Karl Rahner, has two major philosophical works to his credit. Their titles can be read as his two complementary definitions of the human person: *Spirit in the World* and *Hearer of the Word.* The human person, according to Rahner, is spirit but not in the traditional sense of something contrary/contradictory to matter, but as that which is able to transcend the world or observable reality and thus make Metaphysics. The human person is basically a capacity to transcend and reach God, but – and here is the valuable point – we can only be spirit (capable of transcendence) when we are situated in the World. Not only are matter and spirit not seen as the absolute antithesis of each other, in the human person, their very interdependence is underscored. From this it follows that we are called to be "hearers of the Word". In other words, if God freely decides to make a personal self-disclosure to us, God must make this revelation to us *in* the World, the only possible "locus [for us] of the theological event". Humans would only be able to receive and respond to a message from the divinity if it were expressed in the world, that is to say, within history. Hence, the human person must be ever on the alert to listen to a possible addressed to us by God there: we are, by definition, hearers of the Word, God's Word, spoken in the world. And even if God were to freely decide not to utter his Word in the world, then we would attain our fullest self-realisation by listening to the silence of God. Thus both the world and our human bodies, through-which we are rendered incarnate in it, are of paramount importance.

Joseph Maréchal: This eminent Belgian Jesuit, in his *Le point du depart de la Metaphysique*, through his analysis of intellectual dynamism, showed how the human person is driven outside of himself/herself in quest for the fullness of being.[8] Moreover, precisely

8 Joseph Maréchal. 1944. *Le point de départ de la métaphysique: leçons sur le développement historique et théorique du problème de la connaissance*. Bruxelles;

because we are, by nature, seekers of the Unlimited Being, we must immerse ourselves in the world, through our bodies, because, as far as we are concerned, that is the only place where we could encounter God. At this juncture we are reminded of Rahner's telling phrase, "There is no salvation outside the world". We must take the world seriously because it is a participation in God: it is the only context against which we can come to know and love God. And, consequently, we must take our bodies seriously for only an embodied being can seriously get involved with the world. From here it is not too difficult to see how and why humans must take history seriously and live out, within the world, their basic human res-possibility to make it God's Kingdom-a place where God's presence and power is more clearly manifest to all.

Common Parlance: Modern European languages-including the English as we speak it now-are built on roots taken from ancient Greek and Latin. Thus, it is inevitable that some of the slants and biases of the Hellenic world-view should have slipped into our everyday life through the usage of common words. When we use the term "man" (which, significantly is supposed to refer to woman, too), we are saying, in effect, that the most important thing about us is that we have a *mens*, or mind. It would seem that the same emphasis lies behind the Sanskrit *manas* (also mind) and its derivatives like *manushya*. The incarnate dimension of this "mind" is conveniently by-passed, suggesting that "the body" and its needs are of relative unimportance: they key thing is to provide for the needs of the mind or spirit-hence we speak of "spirituality" (as if cultivation of our corporeality could safely be ignored in the quest for human development). On the other hand, the word human implies a far more integrated vision: it reminds us that we are *humus* (Latin: earth, mud) plus *mens* – earthy minds. Here both dimensions are given a balanced stress in a conception that comes very near to Rahner's "spirit in the world".

These examples should suffice to sensitise us to the implications of oppressive and liberative understandings of the human person, against which we can test the potential for all-round human

Paris: L'Édition universelle; Desclée, De Brouwer.

development that any "ism" or concept offers. At the same time, it should be clear,' by now, how these are no mere abstract "airy-fairy" academic discussions, but issues that have a very practical and serious repercussion in the existential order of actual women and men and their struggle for justice and peace.

Some Quotes

"What a piece of work is man! How noble in reason' how infinite in faculty! in form, in moving, how express and admirable! in action how like an angel! in apprehension how like a god! the beauty of the world! the paragon of animals!"

– Shakespeare, *Hamlet*. II, ii, 316.

"The moment I have realized God sitting in the temple of every human body, the moment I stand in reverence before every human being and see God in him - that moment I am free from bondage, everything that binds vanishes, and I am free".

– Swami Vivekananda

"We are born, so to speak, twice over; born into existence, and born into life; born a human being, and born a man".

– Jean-Jacques Rousseau

Chapter 2

BEING AND HAVING

Introduction

These two innocuous and common-place verbs are of key importance in liberation philosophy. Precisely because they are so basic, they have a subtle influence on the way we view things, how we relate to people and whether we take the world seriously or not. In most languages, they function as "auxiliary" verbs, helping us to form tenses or give an idiomatic twist to phrases. Compare, for example, "I have drunk" and "I am drunk"! It is interesting to note that there is, strictly speaking, no exact word for "to have" in Hindi and many modern Indian languages. Where we would say, in English, "I have two eyes", a slight modification of "to be" does the job in Hindi: "To me there are two eyes!" If we think of it a bit, we would recognise that "to have" implies some kind of participation, a kind of analogous form of "to be". Whereas "to be" could imply some kind of identification, "to have" indicates some kind of distancing. Thus, God could say, "I am truth.'! We however, at best, might be able to declare, "I have truth." God could be identified with Truth, of Beauty or Goodness. For us, on the other hand, these are qualities that we share in, but cannot be identified with. This lack of a verb for "to have" is perhaps one of the reasons why the real Indian people, the people of the soil-adivasis, our "aborigines"-settle for a life of simplicity and contentment: there is no subtle brainwashing from the verb "to have" to keep on insinuating how important it is to possess, to accumulate, to "keep up with the Joneses". On the flip side, the dearth of such a verb facilitates the slide into pantheism!

Implications for Liberation

This may all be very interesting. But what has all this "verbal analysis" to do with the philosophy of liberation? Quite a lot. Among other things, it gives us an insight into the anatomy of an unjust society. Putting it bluntly, an unjust society is one where "to have more" takes precedence over "to be more". In other words, these verbs give us a glimpse as to where our values lie, how our lives are oriented, what it is that, deep down, we hunger and thirst after!

In the previous chapter, we recognised that the human person is dynamic, has several appetites or needs that jostle within for fulfilment. Indeed, a thing can be said to have value for us precisely because we perceive it as being able to satisfy some lack or longing. Now, there are two levels of value, two ways in which a thing can do that and these correspond to the two basic types of need in us: the need to *be more* and the need to *have more*. Neither can be ignored. Both must be taken seriously. The question is how to harmonise them and what to do if they conflict or clash with each other.

Our consumeristic society assures us that happiness, self-realisation and peace of mind (call our ultimate goal by whatever name you will) is to be found in *having* more – having more things, having more money or having more power. As a matter of fact, people often judge others in terms of what they have. A common value-judgment (even if it is not verbalised so bluntly) is, "I am a better person than you because I have a bigger bank balance". People tend to look down on the neighbour who has a smaller house, a cheaper car ... or no smartphone! And if someone, after having laboured long to hoard, to amass, to "have more" doesn't yet find that elusive happiness, the Gospel of consumerism assures him/her that it is merely because he/she needs still more – or maybe a more up-to-date model, or the latest fashion! As for sharing-why should I share? If I share, I end up by having less and happiness resides precisely in having more. If "having more" is one's ultimate goal (inasmuch as it is seen as the only way to happiness), then I would be prepared "to be less" so long as it helps me "to have more". So, I would be ready to be less human, less loving, less truthful, less loyal – so long as this would help me to have more. Isn't this what's happening in our capitalistic, cut-throat world? Is it any surprise to us that thought there is more than enough food already in the world (enough, UN statistics tell us, to feed 10% more people than the total population of the earth), almost half the men, women and children alive today go hungry to be each night. The phenomenon of world hunger and other miseries is not so much due to lack of food or other resources: invariably that exists a-plenty. It's a lack of sharing that is the problem.

On the other hand, an authentic philosophy of liberation assures us that fulfilment, peace of mind, happiness consists in seeking to *be more*, growing in humanness and all this involves. It's a question of seeking one's overall human growth, not just one aspect of ourselves at the cost of all others.

Let's take an example. Food is a basic human need – indeed, a basic need of all that lives. We must have food, clothing and shelter-to mention just three "material" needs-in order to live. Thus, "to have" is not bad: if we don't *have* sufficient quantities of certain things, we wouldn't be able to *be* at all The point is that "having" should be subordinated to being: by all means, have as much as one requires to be more. When "having more" begins to clash with one's "being more", it's time to cut down on the having. If I – like the ancient Romans – were to indulge my appetite for food and thereby gorge and stuff myself unlimitedly (stopping by the *vomitorium* to tickle my throat, disgorge the whole mess and surrender myself to the pleasure of gluttony once more), I'd end up by seriously harming my poor stomach! The "joys" of "having more food" would, in this case, end up by frustrating my being more human and confine me to bed. This would effectively put the lid – for a time at least-on my overall human growth. It would be the same, were I to surrender to my urge to "have more" sexual pleasure by raping a helpless woman or molesting a defenceless child. I will assuredly "have more" of what I sought, but I will not have grown "more human" by doing that: I would not have matured in my capacity to love generously and unconditionally! And only if "being more" is my ultimate means to fulfilment would I be prepared to share. For when I share I do *have* less but it could enable me to "*be* more"!

Even in Religious Matters

Many people have even developed what I would call a "capitalistic spirituality". They "do good" not in order to "*be more* human" but to "*have more*" grace! They end up by looking upon their fellows as mere means to increase their heavenly bank balances, their "merit"-and the local currency in heaven, according to them, is called "grace"!

This is that legalistic religiosity which is caricaturised in the Gospels as the "goodness of the Pharisees". There was no love (the sphere of religious "being more") in their lives: it was all a question of fulfilling laws and thereby increasing their "stock" of goodness.

How many clerics and religious-of various creeds-use their "state" as a means to acquire power, give them access to the high and mighty – and cultivate a nice little nest egg! How often parish feasts and novenas are celebrated in such a way that the "keepers of the shrine" accumulate more wealth. "Ours is the genuine miraculous statue," is the claim. Or, "This statue has touched the true relic." The bottom line is: give your donations to us, not to the other rival down the street or in some other pin-code. And ladies with vie with each other to drape the holy idol in the most expensive sari ("I have more devotion than you, for the sari I gave cost more than the one you gave!").

The evil of making "having more" one's supreme guiding light can sneak in anywhere, corrupt the most sublime of all quests and adventures. It is only love that can make sense out of the struggle to "be more"! I think this is what Jesus lived. The famous Christological hymn in Philippians tells us that he did not regard his divine privileges and prerogatives as qualities he had to have and cling to at all cost. In order to more like us, share in every human condition (including death, and not just any old form of death, but the most cruel and humiliating death on a Cross), emptied himself of all such Godly attributes (Phil 2: 4-8). And are not the Beatitudes a call to a life-style based on seeking to *be more* rather than *have more*? It has been remarked that the word, in English, lends itself to a significant pun: "be-attitude", attitude of being!

Three Basic Liberative Attitudes

It was commonplace before Vatican II to refer to religious life, as lived out in the various Orders and Congregations, with the help of "the three vows" as a "state of perfection". Indeed, even the conciliar document on Religious life was entitled "*Perfectae caritatis*" (Latin, "Of Perfect Love"). As if only Jesuits, Carmelites and those of their ilk were called to a "state of perfection" or "perfect charity" while the "mere laity" were expected to settle for the Ten Commandments (as indeed I was told by the Novice Master during my Novitiate)! Even the most cursory glance at both versions of the beatitudes, in Matthew as well as in Lake, makes it clear that they were addressed to the disciples at large and not to an elitist group (cf 5:1 and 6:20 resp.).

Whereas, once the three religious vows or "evangelical counsels" as they used to be called were looked upon as ways of renouncing the wicked world, nowadays we tend to see them as means of liberatively committing ourselves to build up God's kingdom "on earth as it is in heaven". In this sense, we can meaningfully see them as embodying three basic liberative attitudes to things, persons and God. All Christians, indeed, all decent human beings, are called to live in the world with these values or attitudes. Marriage, entry into a religious order, the priesthood or single state-all these must incarnate these basic orientations in a manner commensurate with their lifestyle. But the same attitude is asked of all. And, in a very real sense, we can see them as giving us an insight into three liberative dimensions of accepting the priority of being more in one's life!

Poverty and Things: There is no virtue in poverty, in itself. In fact, poverty, as it exists for the most part, in the Third World, is an evil, the result of an option for having more at any price by some, resulting in the deprivation and dehumanisation of the majority. The religious who prides himself or herself on being "poor" in India would, in reality, have to live on the pavement or inside discarded municipal water-supply pipes, in order to witness credibly to that quality. And that, coupled to the level of food, clothing and medical facilities he/she would have access to would render him/her totally unfit for any apostolic commitment.

Should we not see in "poverty" a not-too-well-chosen shorthand name for that basic liberative attitude to things that we all should inculcate, lest we become enslaved by our possessions. The term, then, would imply a fundamental option for being more, rather than having more or, to put it more simply-but equally demandingly-to use, not love, things! One mode of doing this is to vow a simple lifestyle, to demand no special wages commensurate to one's training or office (and it is hoped that religious do this). Another way is to earn one's keep, have money, possessions and a bank account ... and yet not fall in love with these. In a sense, a person who is surrounded by things, money, and power and yet is not possessed by these can give more eloquent witness to authentic poverty.

***Chastity and Persons*:** We tend to think of chastity as a quality of only those who have not married. But let us not forget that chastity is a Christian and human ideal, even for those who have entered into the state of matrimony. Some time ago, there was a big public outcry against the late Pope John Paul II because he had said that "it is possible for a married man to lust after his wife". Critics were up in arms, vociferously denouncing the Pope for his negative approach to married love- "as if it were possible for a man to rape his wife!" one journalist griped! But the Pope was reminding us of a basic truth that is often forgotten in our chauvinistically inclined world: marriage is not a licence to use your partner as a sexual object. Marriage doesn't give a man the right to exploit his wife sexually according to his whims and fancies. How often do we read of the typical Indian husband who forces himself on his wife, whatever be her frame of mind or condition, often requiring her to submit to his pet perverse erotic dreams! With all due respect to the ancient code of canon law, marriage is not *jus in corpus* (right over another's body). The sexual act, within (or without) marriage must be an expression of love and, as such, must respect the integrity of the other, else It is not chaste! Yes, it is possible to rape one's wife. And, sad to say, many men do that - and not only in India! Just as "poverty" reminds us that things must be used, not loved, so does "chastity" recall to us our responsibility to love persons, not use them. One way of witnessing to this is by loving service of all persons, seeking naught in return, through a vow of chastity or celibacy. But this ideal of love is also to be witnessed to in one's unconditional self-gift to one's spouse. The vow of chastity, lived out in a loving, human way, perhaps more eloquently bears witness to this basic Christian and liberative attitude to persons than can be done in married life.

God and Obedience: The fundamental Christian and liberative attitude to God is to obey him above all other allegiances. True, we must render to Caesar all that Caesar may legitimately demand of us but not that which God alone can ask of us: and only God can ask of us our total and unconditional commitment. This is the force of the first commandment in the decalogue: "You shall have no other God but me". The God of the prophets (of all religions) is revealed as a God of freedom. We should bow down to none other as God because God alone-who makes us free-will value and respect our freedom. All other "gods"-money, sex, the state, whatever – if given one's total allegiance – end up by taking advantage of, abusing and manipulating, our self-commitment.

Some Quotes

"Only that person is truly free and liberated who is striving to live by these basic values and is ever alert to every possible inroad that seeks to detract from their fullness. "One should never put on one's best trousers to go out to battle for freedom and truth".

– Henrik Ibsen, *An Enemy of the People*

"A world founded upon four essential freedoms. The first is freedom of speech and expression - everywhere in the world. The second is freedom of every person to worship God in his own way - everywhere in the world. The third is freedom from want ... everywhere in the world. The fourth is freedom from fear ... anywhere in the world".

– Franklin Roosevelt, Speech 6 Jan 1941

Chapter 3

SOME EPISTEMOLOGICAL PRESUPPOSITIONS FOR A PHILOSOPHY OF LIBERATION

Introduction

Epistemology is that branch of Philosophy which is concerned with human knowledge-its sources and the conditions under which it can attain the truth about reality. Now, one of the most vexing issues in epistemology concerns how we explain the fact that there are other people whose views of reality don't quite square with ours. Scepticism and relativism are easy ways out. The one concludes the human person is totally incapable of attaining any truth at all. The other holds, "to each its own;" there are no absolute truths, what is true for one need not be true for another! The problem is that both these defeatist attitudes are self-contradictory. The sceptic is saying, in effect, that he has been able to attain the truth that humans cannot attain any truth! As for the relativist, his position boils down to saying that he has been able to attain the absolute truth (valid for all people at all times and in all places) that there are no absolute truths. In other words, the sceptic cannot state his position without implying that we can attain some truth for sure and the relativist can only advance his thesis by denying it!

However, the unpleasant fact that stares us in the face is that there are a plurality of theories and opinions in philosophy (and also in theology, in politics and most other disciplines). We live no longer in as rationalistic age as Descartes and Kant (though we haven't quite escaped from the charms of the rationalistic will-o'-the-wisp certitude). We all want to be certain about our convictions, but it is difficult to be so when we come across people who are at least as sincere and intelligent as we are and yet hold diametrically opposite views about the same thing! Is it possible to adhere with conviction to one's own personal views and yet, at the same time, be open to, and respectful of, the convictions of others who don't agree with us? We are less inclined to burn at stake, nowadays, those whose opinions conflict with ours. But how do we react to such troublesome people? After all, the very reason that they disagree with us seems to challenge our pet theories: they are a bit of a thorn in the side of our cherished convictions.

But, must pluralism of theories always be looked on as a defect, as a scandal? Could not absolute uniformity be equally a scandal? And is every pluralism, every difference of opinion, a good thing? Should we be prepared to grant everyone the liberty to uphold propagate and practise just about any and every doctrine that he/she wants? Should I respect the "freedom of thought" of a terrorist, a racist, a fanatic? These are some of the epistemological issues that the philosophy of liberation must come to grips with. This is the concern of the present chapter.

Authentic and Inauthentic Pluralism

The development of disciplines like sociology and hermeneutics have made us aware of cultural relativism and of the element of subjectivity in human knowledge. By cultural relativism is meant that no culture is absolute, that is, should be taken as the norm to judge other cultures. If we have occasion to stand in judgment of certain elements within a particular culture, the norm is not this or that culture against which we would measure the standards of the former, but the human person: does this or that aspect of a particular structure or art form enhance the development of the total human person or does it degrade people? In other words, is it liberative or oppressive? As for the subjectivity feature of human knowledge, this is a healthy corrective against exaggerated and naive views about the objectivity of our sensations and thoughts. No one-except the most arrant of sceptics and relativists (and then they would end up contradicting themselves) would deny that we "objectively" perceive the same reality outside of us (this particular chair, that particular bicycle) but what it means, implies or entails for each of us would be different, depending on our particular point of view, life-style, general background, (which might include things like our age, sex, profession and religion). Sometimes, even our mother-tongue can affect the way we look at objects. These are all elements of what we may, for practical purposes, refer to as "culture". It should be evident enough that nobody can strip away all these elements and view things from the perspective of "pure objectivity" ... no more than we can "subjectively decide for ourselves" whether we are being confronted by an elephant or a grass-hopper!

Now, a pluralism or difference of opinions that arises from one's point of view or from cultural differences is valid enough. This is what I mean by authentic pluralism. This kind of pluralism, according to me, is something good, healthy and to be encouraged. Since no particular culture or point of view is perfect or able to grasp by itself each and every dimension of the myriad-hued richness of reality, cross-cultural exchange and dialogue is rewarding and enriching. Such a shared enterprise would result in the discovery of possible prejudices (how can we become aware of our prejudices except by exchanging views with people whose perspective is different from ours?). Among other things, this would strike a relentless blow against cultural chauvinism: we'd be forced to admit that however much we may be (understandably) enamoured of our own culture, there is yet a lot that we can learn from that of others ... as well as a good deal that we can bring to the other! In this sense, lack of pluralism would be a grave scandal: it would leave us in the morass of our illusions and prejudices and very much restrict the depth and wholeness of our vision of reality!

But there is also the possibility of inauthentic pluralism and, sadly enough, we come across a lot of that nowadays. This comprises those differences of opinion that arise out of selective observation, suppression of those data which would go against our favourite theories (and prejudices), exaggerating those facts that would help us to exalt our private racisms and chauvinistic ideas. This kind of pluralism is not only to be discouraged, it should be fought against!

Not unrelated to this issue is a certain hasty "ecumenism" that is equally to be deplored. This consists of trying to sweep all differences under the carpet and try to make out that "basically we are all saying the same thing", when, to be honest and sincere, we are not! We cannot assert that the Hindu notion of the avatara squares with the Christian doctrine of the incarnation and that both Hindus and Christians are in agreement about the after-life: "it's just that the former call it re-birth and the latter say resurrection!" Only crass ignorance and shallowness of thought could lead one to endorse such naive declarations (and I'm speaking from experience of such well-intentioned "dialogues"). Such an attitude does no service to either point of view nor to inter-religious harmony as a whole. It would be far better "to agree to disagree" and ascertain just where it is that we do part company. This, very likely, would lead to a deeper and more critical appreciation of both one's own and the other's perspective as well as the dismantling of distorted understandings of the latter!

Should our Epistemological Goal be "Better Understanding" or "Certainty"? In order to offset the chances of slipping, unwarily, into an oppressive epistemological stance, we should be on our guard as to whether, in our quest for truth and meaning, our focus is on the attainment of certainty or better understanding. Are we looking for "final answers" or "tentative responses"? All this is not so academic a distinction as it might seem to the uninitiated. In the first place, there is precious little about which we can be strictly certain ("firm assent of the mind without any reasonable fear of being in error", as the Thomists put it). The most important decisions of our life, those choices upon which we found our futures, our peace of mind and our security – such as the choice of friends, our "vocation" or commitment to a life-partner – are not (and cannot!) be based upon absolute certainty and guarantees, but on reasonable risk. Were I to wish to build my life solely "on the secure foundation of reason alone" ... well, that would be most irrational, to say the least! In the first place, such a person would not be able to have a friend, fall in love or choose a career. For only a "reasonable risk" can validate such options. Moreover, if he were to be ruthlessly (and rationally!) logical, he ought not to eat a morsel or drink a drop before he has verified, scientifically, that his food and drink contained nothing poisonous or detrimental to his health. Nor should he climb into a bus without first verifying that the driver had a bona fide licence or that each fellow passenger was not an escaped lunatic or murderer on the run. And, given the ease with which documents can be forged nowadays ... where would it all end? Absolute rationalism now ends up becoming quite impractical! Nor should we imagine that "reasonable risk" would, in any way, dilute the strength of one's commitments. I may be able to rationally prove, without a shadow of doubt, that the three angles of a triangle are equal to two right angles (no more, no less), while I would not be able to demonstrate, with equal guarantee, that my best friend is truly reliable and faithful, but that may not weaken my resolve to gamble my life for his sake (while I would entertain strong reservations to do it for a triangle)!

A further difficulty about "certainty" is that it tends to make one suspicious of those whose views don't tally with yours. If I'm certain that I'm right, then how do I explain the stance of the troublesome dissenter? The temptation to hurl anathemas and scream, "Error has no rights!" is very strong. Besides the feeling of being certain has a kind of complacency about it. I have an answer (if not "the" answer): the issue is closed. In other words, to the extent that I make "certainty" my epistemological goal I begin to move towards a recalcitrant, oppressive stand-point!

It would seem quite a different thing were that goal to be a "better understanding" of reality. That way, I remain open to learn more, to gain from the insights of others whose views may not agree with mine at first sight. My current view, to-date, would be but a response-a word that carries no connotation of closeness, of having arrived at an exhaustive "once-and-for-all" stance. Such an approach tends rather to see a dissenter as someone who could help me towards a better perspective rather than a threat to my personal adherences!

"Weltanschauung" Rather than "Ideology": One's overall-comprehensive philosophical vision should be cast more in the form of a rough, tentative framework than a rigid completed system that has but "to be applied to reality". I call the former a *Weltanschauung* and the latter an ideology. For me, ideology is a bad word. I use it in the sense of a cast-iron, already-worked out set of inter-related ideas. And for many people-some Marxist revolutionaries, as well as some Christian conservatives-that is what their "philosophy" is. And, when they find that reality occasionally refuses to fit the mould, they simply force it to do so or discard such recalcitrant data; the system is what counts for them. This is an oppressive epistemological stance: it has no respect for reality. It aims at foisting a preconceived "vision" onto the scheme of things. On the other hand, a liberative approach is open to an ongoing dialogue with the world. If it comes to pass that one discovers a new nuance or dimension of reality that had not been taken into consideration while formulating one's comprehensive vision, then one modifies the latter, integrating this new perspective. As a result things hold together in a deeper, more insightful manner ... and the world and one's self fall into clearer, more inter-related harmony. It is in this sense that Segundo calls for the application of Heidegger's celebrated "hermeneutical circle" in liberation thought. As many have pointed out, perhaps it would be more accurate to call it the hermeneutical *spiral*, for this interplay between vision and reality results in a progressively deeper grasp of things as the exchange goes back and forth. Needless to say, given the fact that one's envisioning has been the outcome of a progressive dialogue between philosophising and facts, these "changes" would most likely be in the form of minor adjustments and modifications, rather than general overhauling and radical pre-envisioning. This implies, of course, that the process whereby one elaborates his/her philosophical response to a controversial issue should remain all along sensitive to liberative perspectives.

Three Basic Steps: Such a process should go through three basic phases or steps in. order to be true to such demands. First there is the *phenomenological imperative*: one 'should begin by collecting the facts, after a careful observation of the data. One must be careful to take into consideration-as I have hinted earlier-all the relevant facts, including those that would fly in the face of one's preferred theory: One must be on one's guard against capitulating before one's neat preconceived and orderly pre-suppositions, letting pre-interpretation influence the collection of data. When this has been done-and only then then-should one move on to the second phase, the *hermeneutical imperative*. This implies seeking to assemble these facts into an overall, unifying interpretation. There is in us an eluctible drive to see things in one interconnected whole and not merely piecemeal. However-and this is an important point-one must be thorough in the hermeneutical imperative: in other words, we must be open to all interpretations that explain the' facts without distortion or exaggeration and, more often than not, at least two mutually exclusive interpretations emerge. We had an example of this when we sought to interpret, a little while earlier, the data concerning the human person, as per our observations. The fact there was that, though humans have a lot in common with the rest of reality, a closer look at our activities reveals one unique feature: our capacity to transcend the immediate here and now sense data. The hermeneutical imperative obliges us to be open to two possible interpretations of this fact: one, we can do so because we have within us a unique and distinguishing element lacking in, all other observable reality, a human soul; the other is that the same ingredients are to be found within us as in the rest of reality: what enables us to transcend is that these elements have attained a higher degree of evolutionary refinement that makes it possible for us to do what the others cannot-at least not yet! Now, both interpretations explain all the facts, but obviously both cannot be true at the same time. Which of these two valid interpretations are we to opt for? This takes us to the third phase which, at the risk of being misunderstood and seeming irresponsibly cussed, I prefer to call the *heretical imperative*, borrowing the title of one of Peter Berger's excellent and provocative sociological studies of our contemporary situation. The etymological meaning of *haeresis*, the Greek root of "heresy", is *choosing*. In other words, we must take a stand: we can't endeavour to remain indifferent to rival interpretations, we must throw in our lot with one or the other.[9]

9 Peter L. Berger. 1979. *The Heretical Imperative: Contemporary Possibilities of Religious Affirmation*. 1st ed. Garden City, N.Y.: Anchor Press.

But precisely how do we hit upon which of the two is "the right interpretation"? Reason is no help here: there is no question of "proving" one right and the other wrong. We cannot, for instance, in the case I have cited above, dogmatically, claim that "matter cannot transcend, no matter how much it evolves" For, on what basis are we founding that assurance? Of course, we have neither any rational basis for saying it can: one assumption is as good as the other.

What is the criterion to employ in choosing one of the two or more conflicting interpretations? We cannot invoke "evidence", the "criterion of truth": that may be all right when seeking "the truth" in an isolated epistemological question, such as the colour of a particular table or the date of someone's birthday. Here, we are busy with an overall interpretation of a series of inter-connected data. It would seem to me that "the criterion of haeresis" is that a particular interpretation "clicks with" me: it resonates with my value system, with my overall perspective of life and action. This my "value system" or "overall perspective of life and action" cannot, however, be the last word on the subject. It must be open to critique, in turn: does it imply a liberative or oppressive understanding of the human person? Hitler's "final solution" to the Jewish question fitted in with his personal values and life perspective: but these latter were racist, inhuman and, therefore, clearly oppressive. An ongoing and thorough critique of one's hermeneutical stance is a strict requirement of the entire liberative process of philosophising!

From Concepts and Idols to Symbols: As Paul Ricoeur has taught us, philosophy must emancipate itself from an excessively rational bias-which is witnessed to by the penchant for conceptual tools and the hankering for rational arguments or "proofs" as also by questionable presuppositions about the comprehensive (rather than the apprehensive) nature of language. Reason, as we have had occasion to point out already, is – undoubtedly – an important human quality. But reason has its limits. As Blaise Pascal was to remark, tellingly, over three hundred years ago, "The heart has its reasons which the reason does not know". Now, reason works with concepts and concepts emphasise the objective aspect of knowledge. Hence, these very useful tools tend to distance us from the object, enabling us to view it more dispassionately tinder its more universal dimension. Affectivity, whose chief instrument is the symbol, on the other hand, complements the approach of reason and concepts by stressing the subjective angle. In other words, it enables us to focus on how this particular object affects me here and now: it is more concerned with how I am personally involved in reality, what is its meaning (and meaningfulness!) for me. Our rational bias, inherited from the Greeks, via Western culture (especially traditional Thomistic Christian thought) predisposes us to smile indulgently at, and overlook, "emotional", "sentimental" paths to reality. Thanks to our Platonic prejudice, we too would be prepared to grace with the word "knowledge" only that information which has the connotation of universal, necessary and unchanging! Obviously, this "detached spectator" mentality that characterises our "serious, knowledge" goes a long way to reinforcing our uninvolved, sitting-on-the-fence mentality, especially when we contemplate "the mess the world is in": "Don't get involved. It's not our problem. Let them handle it!"

But to see "knowledge" as a detached, intellectual, "head-only" acquaintance with reality is only one way of viewing it. An alternative epistemology, one upheld by both Semitics (the biblical world view) and by classical Indian thought (at least by some significant schools), sees it differently. Knowledge, here, is understood as an intensely personal experience. It is not so much an objective grasp of reality, via the intellect, but more a subjective involvement through a total personal encounter. "Adam *knew* his wife and she conceived and bore a son..." is a typical Genesis formula (emphasis mine). The ancient writer had no hesitation to give the name "knowledge" to that most intimate and personal act of married love. Assuredly, the first man was not merely having some kind of intellectual contact with his partner: knowledge is seen as an extremely personal human act of subjective involvement with someone or something. Again, when Jesus is represented by John as saying, at the Last Supper, "This is eternal life: to *know* you, the one true God and Jesus Christ, whom you have sent", – emphasis mine, once again – he is not talking about some abstract philosophical speculation about the identity of the divinity and its representative. It is, once again, that personal and intimate experience of that is meant. This (w)holistic approach is equally characteristic of classical Indian epistemology and is more liberative, too.

The characteristic of a symbol is that it somehow makes present that which it symbolises: I contemplate a dove and, as I "drink in" its gentleness and serenity, a sense of peace descends upon me. However, a symbol always implicitly affirms that there is more to what it has symbolised than the symbol has been able to present. The dove is not peace, it is not the totality of peace, but it puts me in touch with peace. A symbol merely apprehends what it symbolises, it doesn't comprehend it. Etymologically speaking, to 'comprehend' means to grasp completely, to enclose within one's fist, as it were. To 'apprehend', on the other hand, implies just being able to touch with the finger-tips: there is much more to be experienced, but we have been able to come into personal contact with it. An idol, however, is not so modest in its claims: it pretends to have encapsulated in its entirety that which it refers to.

Now, some people have an idolatrous understanding of how language works. Bertrand Russell, with his (in) famous "picture theory of language" (which he had the good grace to reject shortly after) is a case in point. He believed that words were pictures or mirrors of reality: they were able to capture, within their slender confines, whatever they were pointing to. Indeed, this is the reason why he qualified the language of theology and ethics as "non-sense". Inasmuch as words-both spoken as well as written-were somehow or the other spatio-temporal, they were ideally fitted to deal with realities of a temporal and spatial nature and not things like God and moral goodness!

Significantly enough, the people who have most fallen for the idol theory of language have been religious believers. And they have gone on to blasphemously assert that dogmas-enshrined in verbal formulae-have been able to successfully capture aspects of the divine, exhaustively and thoroughly. So much so, that dogmas were for a long time deemed irreformable, unchangeable and the last word on the subject. This is assuredly an oppressive understanding of language and opens the door to all manner of persecution of the "un-orthodox" who dare express their personal experiences and convictions in phrases that don't echo with monotonous exactitude the formulation of the official party line. Only a symbolic, apprehension-theory of language remains open to the development of dogma. As Karl Rahner puts it, "Dogmas are the starting-point of orthodoxy, not its end-point".

The idolatrous approach to language boosts our propensity for having power over, and controlling, reality. Symbols remind us that there is a dimension of things that eludes us, that escapes our manipulation. Many of us feel happier and more secure to think that, through a covalent "word-picture" we have immured and neatly caged the issue in question. Rationalism, as a cursory glance at the history of philosophy bears out, is never quite at home with freedom. After all, freedom involves unpredictability and the rationalist likes everything to be rationally foreseeable, deductible, predictable' Witness the way a Spinoza or a Leibniz seek to reduce the basic unpredictability of freedom to something rationally calculable! A rationalist bias sits most uncomfortably with a commitment to liberation!

Some Quotes

"The reasonable man adapts himself to the world; the unreasonable one persists in trying to adapt the world to himself. Therefore all progress depends on the unreasonable man".

– Bernard Shaw, *Man and Superman*

"The truth has never been of any real value to any human being - it is a symbol for mathematicians and philosophers to pursue. In human relations kindness and lies are worth a thousand truths".

– Graham Greene

"The strongest thing that any human being has going is their own integrity and their own heart. As soon as you start veering away from that, the solidity that you need in order to be able to stand up for what you believe in and deliver what's really inside, it's just not going to be there".

– Herbie Hancock

Chapter 4

SOME HERMENEUTICAL PRESUPPOSITIONS FOR A PHILOSOPHY OF LIBERATION

Introduction

In 1540, Augustine Steuch (Steuchius), theologian and librarian to the Farnese Pope, Paul III, coined a new phrase which would haunt philosophers down the centuries. It was then that he published his massive Ten Books on the *Perennial Philosophers* or *Concordance of Ancient Philosophers with Christian Theology*. This is the first recorded instance of the epithet "perennial" being accorded to any purely human endeavour. Leibniz was quick to snap up the phrase and spearhead the quest for a "perennial philosophy". Nowadays we smile indulgently at such schemes, especially when they are motivated by the naive attempt to cram every well-known thinker's ideas into agreement with some alleged authority, such as the Bible.

Still, we should be honest enough to admit that everyone (including ourselves) lets themselves occasionally be carried off into a mild flirtation with this notion, so professedly despised. Witness, for instance, Comte's "unity of the sciences", Spencer's "first principles", Santayana's "the realm of being" and Heidegger's "*Sein des Seienden*".

Descartes saw in his cogito what Kant hoped his "Copernican revolution" would do for philosophy: open the door for it to become a "strict science", that is, a systematised discipline in which there would be universal agreement. As Karl Jaspers ruefully put it,

> Nowhere at any time has such a *philosophia perennis* been achieved, and yet such a philosophy always exists in the idea of philosophical thought and in the general picture of philosophy considered over three millennia which becomes a single present.[10]

All this would seem to imply that there appears to be a sort of ineluctable thirst in us for some basic common and perduring *Weltanschauung* and it is so deeply rooted in us that it keeps on re-asserting itself in spite of all efforts to ignore or even stifle it.

One way this urge should *not* be responded to, I think, is to go along with Aldous Huxley who naively sought out the "rudiments" of an "immemorial and universal wisdom" in germinal form, from among "traditionary lore of primitive people in every region of the world, and in its fully developed forms ... in every one of the higher religions."[11] He even went on to assign this character of perduring universality to:

> the metaphysic that recognises a divine Reality substantial to the world of things and lives and minds; the psychology that finds in the soul something similar to, or even identical with, divine Reality; the ethic that places man's final end in the knowledge of the immanent and transcendent Ground of all things."[12]

I think all such attempts to foist any such "Highest Common Factor" doctrine on a recalcitrant public are not only doomed to

---

10 Karl Jaspers. 1968. *The Perennial Scope of Philosophy*. Hamden, Conn.: Archon Books. p. 25. Note that the original German title, significantly enough, is *Philosophische Glaube*. Philosophical Faith!

11 Aldous Huxley. 1946. *The Perennial Philosophy*. London: Chatto and Windus, p. 1.

12 *Ibid.*

failure, but also grossly unfair. For one thing, an equally "universal" and "perduring" case could be made – equally selectively! – for any or all of a series of diametrically opposed theses. Then, all epithets like "primitive" and "higher" are awfully subjective, not to mention bordering on the racist! Again, in many cases, similarity of language masks and conceals real differences in content. And assuredly Huxley is being over-zealous in his determination to find areas of agreement. In the slender quote above, we find him putting on the same plane, for instance, theories that find the soul "something similar to, or even identical with, divine Reality" – no small difference!

For reason such as these, many would prefer to situate what is perennial in philosophy in the great and persistent questions that have ever taxed the human mind, rather than in any solutions proposed to them: "questions unite us, answers divide", Nikolai Hartmann was wont to say. My own contention is that, when all is said and done, it may be more in order to seek perenniality in terms of a more liberative attitude to reality, which would be a necessary pre-condition for any serious and constructive comment on the nature of things. In other words, I recommend a "perennial hermeneutic" rather than a perennial philosophy. Whatever be our background or perspective, we should be on our guard against certain ways of viewing reality which would prejudice the case and do violence to the message it addresses us. This would still leave room for a healthy and authentic philosophical pluralism.

After all, philosophy is-or should be-a humble response to a word that comes to us from reality itself. Indeed, the German language preserves very well the dialogical character of word and response in the terms *Wort* (word) and *Antwort* (answer, or anti-word). Every word spoken calls forth from the hearer a corresponding anti-word, a response. This is that basic, dynamic and ever-developing natural dialogue between person and the world that accompanies us all through life. A "perennial hermeneutics" reminds us of those attentive dispositions with which we should listen to the "voice" of reality, so that our philosophy be truly responsive (*Antwortlich*). I would coalesce all these predispositions into one, an attitude which I would call philosophical respect and we have precious little of it these days.

The Three Canons of Liberative Hermeneutics

These "canons" are nothing more than a spelling-out, into statements about reality, of some of the main implications of a sincere and humble respect for reality. One may, indeed, derive a host of other such canons through a deeper plumbing of this basic attitude. But, for me at least, these are sufficient for the task in hand.

Canon One: Reality is Fundamentally Meaningful. Deep-down, we are all strongly convinced that reality basically makes sense. This conviction underlies all our risk-taking and all our action for justice and liberation. As the celebrated *Dutch Catechism* puts it, "Everything we do is a tender, strong and urgent request put to existence. We want it to be kind to us, to be meaningful for us, in a word, to reveal its purpose."[13] In other words, we can't help feeling that reality has a purpose and this purpose is not inimical to us. It is with a deep sentiment of anger and frustration, of being betrayed and cheated, that we-if ever-find ourselves saying, with Macbeth, "Life is a tale/ Told by an idiot, full of sound and fury,/ Signifying nothing."[14]

But what about Sartre? "The word, absurdity, springs to life, at the moment, under my pen." So writes his mouth-piece, Roquentin,[15] as he suddenly becomes aware that nothing in the visible universe can account for itself: it simply is there, but cannot say why. We are engulfed by a steady stream of things that impudently and shamefully thrust themselves upon us, resisting all our attempts to wrest from

13 *The Dutch Catechism* of 1966 (*De Nieuwe Katechismus, geloofsverkondiging voor volwassenen*; English translation: *A New Catechism: Catholic Faith for Adults*) was the first post-Vatican II Catholic catechism. It was commissioned and authorized by the Catholic hierarchy of the Netherlands. Its lead authors were Edward Schillebeeckx OP, the influential Dominican intellectual, and Piet Schoonenberg, S.J., a professor of dogmatic theology at the Catholic University of Nijmegen (whose works were censured by the Congregation for the Doctrine of the Faith on more than one occasion, because of problematic Christological views). Hoger Katechetisch Instituut (Nijmegen Netherlands). 1969. *A New Catechism; Catholic Faith for Adults, with Supplement.* New York: Herder and Herder, p. 5.

14 Macbeth, act V, scene v, line I7.

15 Jean-Paul Sartre. 1938. *La nausea*, Paris: Gallimard.

them some explanation as to why they are there at all. They loom before us, mockingly, obscenely and meaninglessly and fill us with panic, anger and disgust. And doesn't this prove my point? We cannot "take to" the idea of the essential meaningless and absurdity of all things with sang-froid. It is repugnant to us. No wonder that we make use of several strategies of *mauvaise foi* to evade this awful conclusion. And what is most significant is that not even Sartre was able to live by his own "meaninglessness-thesis"! Though he had attacked all form of love and friendship as meaningless – as veiled forms of sadism or masochism, to be precise – yet he and Simone de Beauvoir lived, in effect, a very loyal and faithful relationship, in a manner worthy of any "bourgeois" married couple. Even in his writings he felt himself drawn irresistibly to a covert admission of the value and meaning of human relations. I am referring not merely to *Bariona*[16] (significantly enough, in this quasi-religious work, Sartre explicitly came out in favour of action for justice); even the last edition of his review *Les temps modernes* was, interestingly enough, broken off, when he found he was describing (between Brunet and Vicaries, in "*Drole d'amitie*") a friendship which seemed to lack the teeniest suggestion of sadism or masochism! Besides, in his mature years, Sartre committed himself to all manner of projects for the benefit of mankind. All this goes to show that, to parody a line of T. S. Eliot, "humankind cannot bear too much absurdity". One could question the Scholastic assertion that the human soul is naturally Christian; it is most definitely unSartrean!

The other type of absurdity is the one recognised by Albert Camus. He believed that the world is ruled by a "cruel mathematics" and that the grave and injustice would swallow up all that is good and noble and true, yet he refused to be cowed down by the hopelessness and helplessness of it all! He called for a response of "courageous despair;" the human spirit must not bow before absurdity but, on the contrary, fight against it and seek to build up a world or justice, love and peace ... even if we know, in our heart of hearts, that the whole enterprise is doomed. Camus illustrates our wresting of meaning out of the jaws of meaninglessness.

16 Jean-Paul Sartre. 1967. *Bariona.* 2e édition, Paris: E. Marescot.

And if there are atheists like Nietzsche, who-unlike Sartre could truly celebrate the death of God as Joyful Wisdom, let us note that they are not rejoicing at the discovery of absurdity! Rather, is it the fact that they are convinced-rightly or wrongly-that only an atheistic world-view can assure us of meaning in life.

The fact that the world is meaningful is not susceptible to rational proof. It is a truth that underlies all we say and do and is rooted in what Karl Jaspers called philosophical faith. It is something that springs to the forefront of one's vision whenever we approach reality with that basic openness and humility which I have called philosophical respect. In Jaspers' own words,

> (Philosophical) faith, it would appear, is immediate, in contrast to everything that is mediated by the understanding. Faith would then be an experience, an experience of the Comprehensive (*das Umgreifende*) that either falls to my lot or does not fall to my lot.[17]

It cannot but fall to my lot if I have that basic attitude of respect for reality. This faith is not unlike the famous First Principles, the attempt to prove which is not only futile but unnecessary. And, however much one might try to deny it theoretically, one finds oneself obliged, in practical life, to ever re-assert it.

***Canon Two: This Meaning is Not so Evident*.** This must be stated straightaway after the precedent. For, granted that reality is meaningful, has an order to reveal to us, we should not hastily assume that we have penetrated its meaning. All too easily we succumb to the illusion of listening to reality: mostly we are but listening to our own selves mouthing our favourite pre-conceptions as we view people and things through our own idiosyncratically-tinted spectacles. Or we wrestle with reality to bring it round to the way we would like it to be. This is philosophical disrespect.

Heraclitus of old seems to have been the first recorded thinker to have recognised that the actual meaning of reality is not so straightforwardly evident. We have to take into consideration,

17 Karl Jaspers. 1948. *Der Philosophische Glaube*. Zürich: Artemis Verlag, pp. 14-15.

not only the limitations of words, spoken or written, but the very "hiddenness" of the depths of things. As this early western hermeneut wrote, "The real constitution of things is accustomed to hide itself."[18] Part of this is due to the clouding that we introduce into the picture inevitably, due to our pre-understanding. Thus, it is also worth our while to recall that "an apparent connection is stronger than an apparent one."[19] This is no mere crass obfuscation of a simple matters it is a healthy corrective to that smug attitude that assures us we have "listened" to its message when all we have done is hastily read off what we were (un)consciously wanting to. "If one does not expect the unexpected, one will not find it..."[20]

It needs both respect and persistence to discover the underlying truth of things. "The lord whose oracle is in Delphi neither speaks out nor conceals; he gives a sign."[21] This sign[22] must needs be interpreted.

Canon Three: All Reality is Mystery. Mystery is a bad word in most technical vocabularies. It is certainly persona non grata in scientific circles. We rejoice at the ever-shrinking realms of mystery before the onslaught of research and experiment. The very suggestion that there should be something essentially and permanently mysterious about the world would probably come across to us as an insult to our intelligence. Science – at least as it is popularly understood – is comfortable with what can be accurately measured, weighed and observed. We have a penchant for "clear and distinct ideas" for "plain and unadorned language" in science; mystery, by definition, is unclear, indistinct and shrouded in poetry. Ludwig Wittgenstein, the Austrian philosopher, while giving nodding respect to the mystical (*das Mystiche*) was wont to hold that "Everything that can be thought at all can be thought clearly. Everything that can be

---

18 Heraclitus, and T. M. Robinson. 1987. *Fragments, Phoenix Supplementary Volume*. Toronto, Buffalo: University of Toronto Press. Fragment 211.

19 *Ibid.,* Fragment 210.

20 *Ibid.,* Fragment 215.

21 Ibid., Fragment 247.

22 I would rather use the term 'symbol" instead of 'sign' here.

put into words can be put clearly."[23] And if, on occasion "language disguises thought"[24] that is all our fault: due to our clumsy and inept handling of this excellent tool. On his title page we read the motto he had borrowed from Kurnberger to serve as a kind of overture to his work: "... and whatever a man knows, whatever is not mere rambling that he has heard, can be said in three words." He does not deny that there is an element "whereof we cannot speak", but would recommend that we "pass over in silence" this entire area.[25] To be fair to him, we must admit that he was later to change his views. But many of us seem to be still at the "early Wittgenstein" phase in our philosophical evolution. The suggestion that there is a core of mystery at the heart of all that exists-even the most empirical of things-is normally taken as just another of those silly things we can expect from philosophers and theologians.

Mystery has fared not too well either in religious circles, thanks to the influence of Hellenistic rationalism on Western thought. Conceptual thinking is just as uncomfortable with mystery as empiricism was, and did its best to make this enfant terrible behave. The authors of the *Dutch Catechism* were well aware of this and summed up at least a century of theologising as follows:

> (It) seems true to say that our capacity for recognising the mystery has in many ways been restricted. This is true even of religious instruction, as may be seen from the way the word mystery was explained in the nineteenth century-and later. Some of us remember definitions from our schooldays. It was common to describe the mysteries of our faith as "truths revealed by God which our reason is 'unfortunately ' not yet able to understand, but which we shall be granted understanding later."[26]

23 Ludwig Wittgenstein. 1992. *Tractatus Logico-Philosophicus, International Library of Psychology, Philosophy, and Scientific Method.* London; New York: Routledge & K. Paul. 4.116.

24 *Ibid.* 4.002.

25 *Ibid.* 7.

26 *Op. cit.* p. 446.

Karl Rahner SJ, the eminent theologian, is quite in agreement with this observation. In *Sacramentum Mundi*, he writes:

> Christian tradition has always attested the experience and doctrine of the incomprehensible God who comes to us in mystery. But it cannot be said that the mystery was always emphasised enough. There was always the danger of regarding God's mystery as something that will be overcome, at least in the beatific vision. ... Moreover, this existence of mystery is usually explained by man's pilgrim state.[27]

The existence of mystery was reluctantly admitted. But it was relegated to the level of a temporary inconvenience that we had to put up with in this "vale of tears", due to original sin.

Of course, nowadays many a thinker has done his bit to restore mystery to its rightful place in human experience and discourse and the French existentialist, Gabriel Marcel, is in the forefront of these. In his Being and having, he quotes a sentence from Jouve which could well serve as the leitmotif for the entire Marcellian corpus: "Mysteries are not truths that lie beyond us; they are truths that comprehend us". Defining metaphysical thought as "reflection trained on mystery", he goes on, in a classical and oft-quoted passage, to make his celebrated distinction between problem and mystery:

> A problem is something met with, which bars my passage. It is before me in its entirety. A mystery, on the other hand, is something in which I find myself caught up, and whose essence is therefore not to be before me in its entirety.

In short, a mystery is a question of which I am a part. "A problem is something which I meet, which I find complete before me, but which I can therefore lay siege to and reduce". Whereas "a mystery is something in which I am myself involved, and it can only be thought of as *a sphere where the distinction between what is in me and what is*

27 Karl Rahner. 1968. *Sacramentum Mundi: An Encyclopedia of Theology*. 6 vols. London: Burns & Oates. Vol IV, *Op. cit.* p. 134. He writes in an article entitled, "Mystery."

before me loses its meaning and its validity".[28] One of the reasons why it is not possible to probe a mystery exhaustively and depict it in adequate language is because the elusive me is part of the very data and it is not possible for me to detach myself from this data for objective study!

And yet, when all is said and done, the distinction between problem and mystery can readily blur. This is because every question can be viewed by me from both the perspective of problem as well as of mystery. I can even study myself as an object, as something placed outside of me, in opposition to me as subject! And even the most mundane of questions can be approached from the viewpoint of mystery.-This can happen in two ways, either by "standing far back" or by "zooming down". These two moments of metaphysical reflection highlight the essential mysteriousness of the real.

There is, first' of all, what we might call the ontic stance: this is when we view any reality from the standpoint of being, being as being, as Aristotle would put it. Once we do that, we are plunging ourselves into a dimension of the real in which we are personally involved. For, to return to Marcel, "We are involved in being; it is not within our power to withdraw; put very simply, we are, the question is to know how to situate ourselves with regard to the fullness of reality". Since "being" is not something which we can break down into something simpler to study in a detached manner, we are brought face to face with the recognition that we are caught up in a mystery each time we view something from the perspective of being, or, which is to say the same thing, from the viewpoint of the "transcendental" which are "convertible with being", as the Scholastics say. This has led Marcel to define being as simply "that which resists exhaustive analysis". Man tramps off into the world with his natural penchant to analyse, penetrate and break things down into "abstract elements" which are "thinkable" in terms of "general thought". Suddenly he is stopped short. Something resists the analysing machine. He has come face to face with the ontological mystery. We might as well call this the approach of communion, the recognition of *co-esse* (being with). "The incarnation is the central datum of metaphysics". (*Being and*

28 Emphasis in the original.

Having) In his *Metaphysical Journal.* Marcel had already noted that "reflexive thought (*la pensee pensente*) is a thought that is incarnate in, or involved with, a body and, through it, with being".[29] In fact, so intimate is this bond, this communion, that Marcel goes so far as to ask whether we are justified in making an essential difference between the kind of union we see in "body and soul" and the soul and all other existing realities.[30] Now this experience of communion, of co-esse, of incarnation which, as we have noted, is the primary datum of metaphysics, is the first way that opens us to the horizon of mystery when we contemplate any being.

But there is another movement. We may call it "zooming in", borrowing an image from cinematography. This is when we view a being from the aspect of its individuality. Now, *omne individuum est ineffabile*-the individual resists exhaustive description. It is not just the deficiencies of one's vocabulary and the very limitations of speech in general that make it so. It is the very unrepeatable uniqueness of it which eludes us at every turn and twist of the intricate labyrinth of exploration that we must engage in as we seek to understand it better. This is even more so when we remember that there is no being which is totally inert, static. All the more when we are concerned with living, organic being-and most of all when we are face to face with that "most mysterious of mysteries", the person! We could also speak of this stance as the "bracketing" (pace Husserl!) of *co-esse*, the intercommunion. This does not, however, imply that we are denying it: it is just left in temporary suspension.

So we see that whether we consider things in isolation or as intimately participating in, or rather in communion with, each other, we are beset with mystery. Of course, along with Marcel, I do not mean to imply that there is no real difference between the revealed mysteries of religion and ontological mysteries. The same term is used not only because, as Marcel would have it, "the supernatural must needs have some point of insertion into the natural, without in

29 Gabriel Marcel. 1952. *Metaphysical Journal.* London: Radcliff, p. 10.

30 *Ibid.*, p. 11.

the least implying that it 'is a kind of blossoming forth of it."[31] Also because the ontological mysteries in which we are daily bathed, are but ontological participations in the Ontological Mystery. There is also a circuminsession of mysteries.

Some Quotes

"To see a World in a grain of sand,
And a heaven in a wild flower,
Hold Infinity in the palm of your hand,
And Eternity in an hour."

– William Blake, "Auguries of Innocence"

"Wouldst thou" – So the helmsman answered.

"Learn the secret of the sea?
Only those who brave its-dangers
Comprehend itş mystery!"

– H. W. Longfellow, "The Secret of the Sea"

"Homo sum; humani nil a me alienum puto."
("I am a man; I reckon nothing human alien to me")

– Horace (Latin Poet), *Heauton Timoroumenos*

31 Gabriel Marcel. 1949. *Positions concretes du mystere onto-logiaue.* Paris: Vrin, p. 90.

Chapter 5

THE CENTRE AND THE PERIPHERY

Introduction

We are born into a world in conflict. Discussion there might be as to who, today, are the actual protagonists in this clash: economic classes (as per Marxism), geopolitical groups (the "first world" West vs the "second" world East), the "more industrial" North vs the "agricultural inclined" South, or whether it's more a question of gender or colour splits-the fact is that, whether we realise it or not, from the moment we utter our first cry on earth, we are forced to take sides in a global battle. How truly did Matthew Arnold write, in "Dover Beach":

> ... we are here as on a darkling plain
> Swept with confused alarms of struggle and flight,
> Where ignorant armies clash by night.

Most of us are not aware of the battle going on, for we are not among its prime victims. We climb onto buses (or into cars and rickshaws) to make our way to work or study. We get our newspapers and meals more or less on time. We are able to take regular baths and have our clothes laundered for us. We can go for an occasional movie, party or "night out with the boys"– or simply watch our favourite soap on TV. Not often do we notice that things are not so simple for a sizable proportion of our fellow-citizens or our "fellow-travellers on space-ship Earth". Few of us realise that they are being systematically and forcibly deprived of their rightful share of the cake, because this would make a dent in the abundance of what has been appropriated by the privileged few.

> From Heraclitus to Earl von Clausewitz and Henery Kissinger, "war is the origin of everything", if by "everything" one understands the order or system that world dominators control by their power and their armies. We are at war – a cold war for those who wage it, a hot war for those who suffer it, a peaceful coexistence for those who manufacture arms, a bloody existence for those who are obliged to buy and use them.[32]

A Brief History of Colonialism

Centres Old

During the first millennium or so of recorded history, the Mediterranean emerged as the first great Centre to oppress and exploit its far-flung Periphery. The Greeks and Romans believed they were at the centre of the earth, in more senses than one, and set out to take possession of the rest of the known world. It was these pristine colonial powers who would decide just how many rights and privileges should be enjoyed by the denizens of the remote, inconsequential, "non-civilisations", whose ownership they would dispute among themselves until Rome reigned supreme and unchallenged. Roman law and polity would also provide a blue-print for the more sophisticated colonisers of the future.

For the "Mediterranean millenium" came to its end. Our modem-age began with other European nations taking over where the Greco-Romans had left off. The former had done their homework well: they had learned from the latter that rule number one for any would-be successful colonial power was *divide et impera*: encourage divisions among the subjugated people. Make them aware of their

---

32 Enrique Dussel. 1985. *Philosophy of Liberation*, trsl. from the Spanish by Martinez and Morkovsky, New York, Orbis Books, p. 1.

religious, cultural and linguistic divides. Foment feelings of suspicion and distrust across these borders. For as long as a colonised people remain split into a motley crew of rival ethnic groups, the suzerainty of the foreign "mother country" would remain unchallenged. There were some bloody skirmishes (on colonial territory, never in Europe) between the British, the Dutch, the Portuguese, the Spaniards and the French but it was soon over. The Spaniards had their flag planted firmly on the South American continent, the British were firmly ensconced in Asia (with enviable footholds in Africa, North America and elsewhere) and the, French, Portuguese and Dutch had to lick their wounds and settle for the left-overs.

It was extremely awkward for these intrepid explorers and discoverers that these "New Lands" had old owners and these "aborigenes" had already explored and discovered their own homeland centuries before. This embarrassment was easily dealt with. When the Spanish colonialist raised the question, "Are the Amerindian humans?" he was voicing a perception of the problem common to all colonialists of whatever age or ilk. The implication was that the natives were not Europeans and so could hardly be counted as persons, as rational animals. Hence they had no dignity or status other than what the good Europeans should assign them and whatever they had discovered, explored or named did not count. Europeans would be the first discoverers and explorers of these vast regions. Europeans would "take possession" of these countries and name their lakes, forests and mountains after their sovereigns-Lake Victoria, Maryland and so on. Henceforth, there were no "free gifts of nature": everything belonged to the Europeans (however late they may have arrived on the scene) and to their rulers.

Of course, the wretched "savages" were not too happy about their being "discovered" and "civilised" by the later arrivals. Especially since this involved the latter taking possession of the land, waters and the air that they had always assumed were the property of their ancestors, themselves and their descendants. This necessitated the unpleasant interlude of having to get rid of these ungrateful and uncooperative wretches. As Bartolome de Las Casas, the early liberation thinker was ruefully to sum up the behaviour of his contemporaries: "They have used two ways to extirpate these pitiable nations from the face of the earth. One is by unjust, cruel, bloody and tyrannical wars. The other is ... the most violent, horrible and hateful slavery". In that brief comment we have summed up for us the Centre's persistent policy for dealing with the periphery. The methodology nowadays is less bloody and violent, but nonetheless effective and devastating. At first there were wholesale decimations and massacres of the people of the periphery – sometimes, as in the case of North America, by making and breaking "peace treaties" as when pragmatic conditions dictated, sometimes by betrayal and deceit, as in Pizarro's conquest of Peru and sometimes by the simple expedient of supplying raw meat to the aborigines as in Australia and New Zealand. Later, the Centre learnt that it would beexpedient not to kill of everyone: women, children and some able-bodiedmen could profitably be kept on to do the dirty work as slaves.

As the world became more "enlightened" and "humanised", colonialism got a bad name. Besides historical circumstances conspired against the costly business of maintaining outposts away from home, especially when their erstwhile submissive subjects had begun to assimilate dangerous and subversive democratic ideals. But, as Vatican II puts it, about our times, "At no time have men had such a keen sense of freedom, only to be faced by new forms of slavery in living and thinking."[33] The pattern seems to be: colonialism is out, other forms of tyranny are in. STAR TV and other international media provide a subtle form of cultural domination which is already resulting in more or less overt expressions of pedagogical and sexual domination. The "free" market economy and multi-nationals seek to complete the process. Thus millions of men, women and children-together with their life-styles-were sacrificed to the newly emerging Molochs of mercantilism, immolated on the altars of the almighty dollar or the pound sterling. Colonialism-in its classical form as well as in its twentieth century varieties – ended up recording more human sacrifices to their Supreme Beings than the old "savages" had to their traditional gods-a practice that was deemed horrible by the civilised Christian Europeans.

33 *Documents of Vatican II,* "The Church in the Modern World," No. 4.

History is written by the conquerors and they invariably write it to justify their excesses and tyrannies. So they saw to it that the "pre-colonial natives" were represented as uncouth, immoral brutes with no culture, no religion worthy of the name and no real human feelings. This was a gross travesty of the facts, as any contemporary scholar of Comparative Religion could have told them. But that was no major problem for the early colonial historian. From there it was but a small step to the conclusion that the "white man's burden" laid on his noble shoulders by his white man's God was to educate, civilise and Christianise these poor savages as best as he could. In effect, this would involve Europeanising them as much as was humanly possible-making all due allowances for their inferior capacities! Macaulay's recommendation was that the best form of education for Indians would be to make them all "brown Britishers", by-passing the wealth of the Vedas and the entire gamut of Indian culture, which he dismissed as ridiculous and unworthy of human attention. Thus the biased historian could conclude that colonialism was the best thing that could have happened to the poor devils. Indeed, the European conquerors saw themselves as having done the natives a favour by colonising them, replacing their sub-human culture, value systems and speculations with the noble language, art and religion of their liberators!

Philosophical Presuppositions

It would seem that, for the colonialists (and their latter day variants), the old Cartesian bedrock, *cogito ergo sum*, would have to be replaced by *conquiro ergo sum* (I conquer, therefore, I am). In other words, it would no longer be the ability to think (cogito) that guaranteed one the rights of human existence (*ergo sum*) but the fact that one had come out on the top, had conquered. Only the conquistador had the rights and privileges of human existence. The rest – the vanquished native – did not. He or she could be enslaved, made a concubine or thrown to the lions for sport. One was not honour bound to keep one's word to such non-persons. And, since the colonisers' womenfolk and children had no direct part to play in the great act of conquering, it was no surprise that they could enjoy, at best, only limited rights and privileges. Females would never know full rights;

males could provided that, when they came of age, they played their part in conquering or administering the subjugated people. In the long run, it was not one's ability to cogitate, to build up a mighty civilisation such as that of the Aztecs or be courageous hunters as the Amerindians or elaborate impressive philosophical systems as the Hindus, Buddhists or Muslims: all that mattered was that one be a conquering warrior. If one did not show himself capable of that, all his other accomplishments counted for nothing.

As we humans became more "enlightened" and old forms of colonialism collapsed, new kinds of colonialism and oppression arose-a more subtle and refined version, but no less deadly in effect. Just as Christians had learned to replace bloody and gory human sacrifices with the "unbloody" sacrifice of the Mass, so too the conqueror became less bloody and his oppression of the non-white, non-conqueror continued-and, sometimes, even intensified-but in less bloody manifestations. Of course, bloody wars did not cease altogether: napalm, Kalashnikovs and Exocet missiles and their ilk would replace swords, bows and arrows of yester century. Yet the more common, more prevalent battles and conquests would be carried on by other, more sophisticated and less evidently offensive ways. Thanks to the "global", "free" market and the capturing of the media by powerful First World moghuls, cultural, linguistic and social domination would continue in a most destructive and effective the diminishment – if not the total annihilation – of native identity and its replacement by the white man's superior culture and identity.

Long ago, Parmenides – another white man! – had enunciated his basic metaphysical conviction: "Being is; non-being is not!" The colonists readily agreed. Only the conqueror could merit the title of Being; the vanquished native, by that very title, was 'non-being' and, together with his culture could claim no right to exist. Later on, when "home-rule" became the order of the day, the "local" authorities would ape the values and attitudes of their former Masters. They would emerge as the new conquering class and-with rare exceptions-would do all they could to ensure that only their families, tribe or clan have access to the Conquerors' Club. Structures, laws and customs would be bent, re-interpreted or simply changed to restrict admission to the Club. Prophetic figures would arise from time to time, but the Club perfected ways and means to either eliminate them (with religious approval!) or to ensure that they be taken not too seriously. The embarrassing part of it all that many of these "dead and gone" personages refused to be that: like the proverbial "thorns in the side" they had this disconcerting habit of "living on" in the nonentities they fought for and "conscientised". Worse still, some highly respectable candidates for the Conquerors' Club refused to seek membership, spurning all preferred privileges and opted to "go over to the natives", even to the extent of identifying with them and their demands. The wheel had now come full circle: no longer were the non-white natives being subtly compelled to become "brown sahibs"-or black or yellow one's for that matter, the white sahibs were freely opting to become non-brown natives! Liberation was catching on.

But this did not upset the Conquerors' Club for long. After all, as they say, "If you can't lick 'em, join 'em!" And so the authorities appropriated liberationist vocabulary and slogans. The most repressive regimes would call themselves "free" or "democratic" or "peoples'" republics and larded their political parties and action groups generously with such misleading epithets. The most autocratic dictator would intersperse his harangues with platitudinous mouthings about equal rights, the protection of minorities and concern for the downtrodden (even if it was his underlings who were doing the down-treading in the first place). Classic examples of this may be found in expressions like "free" market economy and a society based on "free" love, where the only people who were free in these set-ups were the powerful in the face of the helpless, liberation thinkers had to learn to be wary of those who use liberationist jargon.

Hobbes' adage, *homo homini lupus* (man unto man is like a beast) was meant to be a sad description of the deplorable state of affairs in primitive, uncivilised nature. It is more an accurate summary of the contemporary political application of the Cartesian cogito.

Centres New

Northatlanticism: The vagaries of history have concentrated the most powerful and wealthy nations in the same strategic area: all along the Northern shores of the Atlantic Ocean-on both sides of it! On one side looms today's only super-power, the United States, fortunate enough to have been able to build its economic and financial might by wresting a wholly untapped source of natural wealth from the natives. On the other is England and its colonial rivals, all gorged with the booty and resources expropriated from Southern-based colonies. Together with the Scandinavian nations (with these playing a relatively minor role in the process), they would call the rules of the game and the ravaged and disadvantaged South would have no choice but to obey. Extermination was out, but a judicious level of under-nourishment was in. This would ensure the dependence of former vassals whose existence was useful to the Masters, inasmuch as they performed essential tasks, provided necessary imports ... or afforded convenient sites for messy, polluting industries that could not be established "back home" without running foul of pro-ecology laws. Out of this network of inter-locking, mutually supportive decision-makers came the pattern for a more industrial North to set the standards for a more agricultural South. This same style was parodied within the very economically disadvantaged nations of the South, leadership invariably came from the Northern States or Provinces and their language, art forms and interests dominated those of their Southern neighbours. And, when these, in desperation, started regional political parties and other pressure groups to protect their cultural Identity from being swallowed up by the Northern Leviathan, these were accused of being narrow and "provincialistic"! But what other chance did they have, otherwise? No one seemed to have thought of that question. And maybe we should move towards a more federal, less centralised form of Government after all!

Many "Worlds" in "the World": In his insightful and provocative encyclical, *Sollicitudo rei socialis* (December 30, 1987),[34]

---

34 Pope John Paul II. 1988. *Encyclical Letter Sollicitudo Rei Socialis of the Supreme Pontiff, John Paul II, to the Bishops, Priests, Religious Families, Sons and Daughters of the Church and All People of Good Will for the Twentieth Anniversary of*

Pope John Paul II made reference to the sad fact that we can speak of "different worlds within our one world: the First World, the Second World, the Third World and at times the Fourth World". (No 14) We are more or less familiar with the first three. The former two are taken, in common parlance, to comprise the "developed" nations, the last the "developing" one's. The First World is more or less co-extensive with Northatlanticism and assembles the so-called "free" (non-communist) wealthy nations of the West. After the collapse of the Iron Curtain and the dismemberment of the former USSR, the term "Second World" has become somewhat outdated. It was meant to sum up all those East European countries that had been "swallowed up by the Russian bear" as well as China and those Northern parts of Asian lands that had also succumbed to Communism. These latter, admittedly, were not as prosperous as the First World "models" (and now we realise that they were a good deal worse off than they pretended to be) but claimed to be an alternative model of development, more "proletarian-based" than the other capitalistic varieties. Just for the record, I mention here that the Pope, in the above document, rejected both models of development, that of "liberal capitalism" as much as that of "Marxist collectivism" as neither took the total human person as its inspiration: but more of this, later. This brings us to the Fourth World which, as the related footnote (No 31) tells us "is used not just occasionally for the so-called less advanced. Countries, but also and especially for the bands of great or extreme poverty in centuries of medium and high income". I would rather use the phrase to refer to those pockets of glaring poverty that are to be found among the wealth and opulence of First and Second World nations as also pockets of nigh-unparalleled opulence found among the poverty and squalor of the Third World.

Urban Centres and Rural Peripheries: This is the set-up that is "at work" in India. Decisions are made by and for the city elites who see to it that budget outlays, plans and projects are allocated and opted for on the basis of what promotes their own self-interest or provides

---

Populorum Progressio. Washington, D.C.: Office of Publishing and Promotion Services, United States Catholic Conference, 1988.

them with more sophisticated luxuries and toys, and not whether these would assure basic necessities to deprived rural people. Thus, when the question of switching from black-and-white to colour TV came up during the Asian Games in Delhi, there was little hesitation in approving the expense-even though the same funds could have been used to give clean drinking water facilities to villages that had been suffering immensely due to this lack. If a "plague" breaks out in an important urban area like Surat, the administration swings into action and ensures that the disease is dealt with swiftly and eradicated, so efficiently that we are told that, that former "plague-ridden" city is now a model of hygiene and sanitation. Similar-and worse-problems have plagued (the choice of the word is deliberate) many villages since before Independence ... and they remain. The situation has become so mockingly grim that social analysts speak of India (the big cities and their suburbs) and Bharat (the villages and rural areas of our land) as two separate nations and, they go on to add, tongue-in-cheek, we often come across refugees from Bharat, living in India, hoping to better their prospects. India throws them a few scraps, exploits their services ... and from time to time demolishes their hovels as part of a beautification of India scheme. The pattern is repeated in many another Third World nations.

"Big" and "Little" Traditions: Just as the Centre has its history, art and tradition, so does the periphery. But, as in all such matters, the former dominates the latter. Indeed, it does this so effectively as to identify its culture with that of the entire nation, region or group. The "other" cultures and traditions, by that token, are reduced to the status of monocultures, non-traditions. In other words, side by side with-the very eloquent styles of music, dance and painting-whose development and publicity are encouraged and fostered with generous grants, not to mention a substantial amount of occasional "foreign aid"-there is a "culture of Silence", which desperately struggles to keep alive. This is the "folk" dance, the "folk" art and so on of the tribals, dalits and other underprivileged and economically disadvantaged groups. There is scant hope of the "Centre" releasing funds for the preservation and development of such forms of culture. This expression of art is ignored, falls silent and dies off. In Latin America, many of the ancient tribal languages are disappearing and

Spanish is replacing native languages. The same things are happening in India, too.

Very often our attempts at Inculturation-laudable enough in themselves-are not properly geared towards liberation. It is often the "big", "oppressive" or Brahmanic tradition that we draw upon in the liturgy. We are accustomed to use Sanskrit (replacing one incomprehensible dead language, Latin, with another, more incomprehensible one which died perhaps even earlier), the sacred language of the hated Brahminic oppressors of the dalits. In Pathardi, a mission station not far from Pune, where the local Christians are dalits, priests discard the usual saffron-coloured shawl in favour of green one, for the same reason. Wearing a saffron vestment would identify them with the oppressive priestly caste in the eyes of the very persons we wish to liberate! There seems to be no dearth of priests and religious who study and become expert in classical dance forms, or music, as well as, of course, the great brahminic philosophical traditions. How many are there who, like Wendell D'Cruz sj, have studied katkari art and are saving it from extinction? We should ensure that our Inculturation merges with our option for the poor and seek to inculturate the "culture of silence" into our liturgy and aimm to conscientise the poor, making them aware that their art is truly art-as much as Bharat natyam and as worthy of study, even at an international level-as the more well-known "Indian" classical forms.

Some Quotes

"He that despises small things, will fall little by little." –Eccl. 19:1
"Small is beautiful." – Erich Schumacher

"Unless you turn about and become like little children, you will not be able to enter the Kingdom of Heaven." – M*t* 18:3

"It has long been an axiom of mine that the little things are infinitely the most important."

– Arthur Conan Doyle, *The Memoirs of Sherlock Holmes*

"The small things of life were often so much bigger than the great things . . . the trivial pleasure like cooking, one's home, little poems especially sad ones, solitary walks, funny things seen and overheard."

– Barbara Pym

"You need to let the little things that would ordinarily bore you suddenly thrill you." – Andy Warhol

Chapter 6

TOWARDS THE LIBERATION OF RELIGION

Introduction

Religions – and their offshoots, theologies – have not always historically proved themselves reliable friends of liberation. The subjugation of woman has often been given their sanction. The most cruel and bloodthirsty wars have been fought in the name of religion and *Gott mit uns* (German: God is on our side!). Religion has often opposed scientific research and sided with obscurantism and superstition against trends of enlightenment. And politicians have learned that religion is the easiest handle by which people can be manipulated ino all manner of brute mob action in favour of building vote banks. Indeed, religious leadership is the one surviving bastion of male exclusivism that is determined to hold out against "feminine incursions" and reserve its power to men only. The priestly Conquerors Club is a very powerful and jealously guarded coterie which clings, with bull dog like tenacity, to its ever shrinking list of privileges and prerogatives. Above all, it flashes its wand of "God's will" and the "divinely willed scheme of things" to justify the status quo and preserve many an unjust and questionable structure-secular and religious-that might (?) once have been justified but which nowadays is more a hindrance than a help to humans encountering God. On the other hand, we cannot deny that religion has inspired many to selfless service, especially of the down-trodden, has given the human race a rich legacy of art and beauty and has played a not insignificant part in opening our eyes to the essential dignity of the human person, irrespective of race, colour or sex. Some Churchmen and not a few valiant women-believers have been a friend to liberation.

Oppressive "Gods" and the Liberative God

The Basis of Religion

At the onset, let me dispel any possible notion that I am going to identify the "god" of one religion as liberative and the presiding deities of all others as oppressive. Far from it. My contention is that every religion-and each of its doctrines-are 'susceptible to a liberative as well as an oppressive interpretation. Indeed, there is such a thing as oppressive and liberative atheism. It's all a question as to whether the enhancement of the total human person is being sought or not. Thus, within the same religion, we might identify people who worship an oppressive "god" and those who personally encounter the liberative One in the experience of a mystical encounter.

Sadly enough, for many people, it is observance of code, creed and cult-necessary expressions of all organised religion-that is taken as the basis of religion, instead of mystical experience (which is not so esoteric and unattainable as most people think). All that the latter requires, on our part, is an attitude of humility, of openness, "the heart of a little child". All this is difficult only because it is so easy. And the more one is learned, the more "faithful" one tries to be in performing one's "religious duties", the bigger is the danger of mistaking the, pointer for the reality and tumbling into the rut of spiritual pride and intolerance-occupational hazards of all those who seek to be truly religious.

In fact, it is the religious fanatic – whose mind and spirit is too far removed from that of the little child to be open to a genuine encounter with the *ganz Andere*, the Wholly Other – who usually becomes the self-appointed over-zealous and merciless enforcer of the unholy trinity of code-creed-cult, his tyrannical divinity (the masculine pronoun is intentional).

Creed is a summary list of doctrines to which all followers of a particular religious body are expected to give their qualified assent. Failure to do so would risk one being termed "heretic", "schismatic", "infidel", "gentile" or whatever is the current term of opprobium in the reigning fanatics' vocabulary. Once upon a time, such qualifications would lead straightaway to a death sentence: being led to the stake, hanged, drawn and quartered, removed from the land of the living by a fatwah or a variety of other ingenious methods, specially invented for the occasion by the local zealots. In our "enlightened" times, the fanatic has to reluctantly settle for more "unbloody" solutions, ostracism, withdrawal of one's licence to teach, excommunication. Of course, the believing community has every right to decide which enunciations of faith-convictions authentically express the common beliefs of the community. And the believing community has every right to censure or qualify as inauthentic certain irregular formulations. But it should be the community or a truly representative body of the community that sees, judges and acts-not an over-centralised, isolated and self-propagating select band who are closed to the development of dogma, other cultures, points of view and perspectives. Such executive-legislative-judiciary power should not be allowed to accumulate solely in the exclusive hands of an inbreeding European Conquerors' Club (which may include in the ranks a few well-chosen, properly brain-washed old men from the periphery).

Code comprises all those moral rules and derived customs that members of "particular organised religions are supposed to follow in their daily life. These may include certain styles of dress, proscriptions of certain forms of food and drink, prescribed "holy days" for worship or "pentitential times" of fast and so on. All religions generally agree on basic moral principles as respect for elders, not taking the life of an innocent person, not stealing and so on. There is difference, however, on certain controversial areas as birth-control, the use of violence in times of war and so on. There was a time when religions were so immediately linked with State policy that any contravention of the religious code was viewed as a treasonous act against the State and the culprit was handed over to the secular arm for punishment. Nowadays, most religions have voluntarily or involuntarily relinquished such connections and have to content themselves with at the most, issuing moral condemnations against offenders and appealing them to mend their ways. Some form of ostracism and/ or excommunication is often visited on the incalcitrant. One might mention, in passing, that penal sanctions for infringements of the religious code, where enforceable, have always been (and continue to be) rather inhuman and cruel, to say the least.

Cult refers to the various rules and rubrics that govern how the "official" (individual or communitarian) worship is to be carried out. This includes a host of things such as what vestments the officiating person is to wear, who is the legitimately recognised officiant for such occasions, what exact words may be used, what symbolic and other objects are to be employed in the event. The degree of meticulousness laid down for some or all of these elements varies from religion to religion. Very often, it is required that the service be performed in the language that was current when that religion first saw the light of day. Very often this entails the usage of a dead – or, in other cases – a foreign language, in any case, one unknown to the majority of the devotees. This requirement, among other things, ensures that only legitimately empowered persons preside over the rites (for only they would have been able to spend several years mastering that relatively unknown form of communication). The usual proscriptions are threatened against all who do not observe these laws. In most cases, the worship is declared "invalid" (null and void) if some or all of the details are not carefully observed.

Why Organised Religion?

Disgusted by the amount of "soulless repetition" that is carried on in the name of religious worship, many believers-especially the youth (who being dynamic and creative, abhor monotonous recitals of old formulae and dull re-enactments of meaningless gestures), question the relevance of organised, institutionalised religion. Why join one of the formally constituted religions and be obliged to put up with its irrelevant panopoly of code, creed and cult? Why not live a decent human life, be of service and help to others and worship God privately at home? This is undoubtedly one possible solution to the problem. What we must-ask, however, is whether this "solution" doesn't, of itself, create another problem-perhaps one even greater than what it tried to solve! For we are social beings, as much as individuals, by nature, and it would be detrimental to our overall development to ignore one of these vital facets of human life, in any sphere. Thus, in a close friendship, were I to rigidly enforce my exclusive will on my friend, requiring him/her to bow before my every whim and fancy, I would destroy my friend, our relationship and, by that token, harm myself (for none of us can live without human companionship). On the other hand, were I to do just the opposite, capitulating before my friend's desires, I would equally annihilate a precious aspect of myself (my unique, personal and irrepeatable identity). Life is invariably a matter of learning to find a delicate balance between extremes such as these.

Now, in relating to God, I also have an individual and a social dimension that must enter into the picture, lest I leave an essential part of myself unfulfilled and frustrated. Just as I am naturally and spontaneously driven to express my deep feelings about anyone or anything that is special to me (my close friend and my country, respectively), in both and individual and in a societal manner, so too does my religious faith need an individual as well as a societal expression! On the occasion of a close friend's birthday, I am moved to express my personal love for him/her by an individual greeting, a gift and exchange of words-but I also want to celebrate my love for him/her at a birthday party with the larger group of family, friends and acquaintances. Nor am I satisfied by a kind of individual and private love for my country: my patriotism drives me to rallies and parades where, together with my other loyal fellow citizens, I salute the flag and sing the national anthem. In the same way, authentic religious devotion cannot find its fulfilment only in personal and private prayer: it must need also spill over, from time to time, into liturgical or communitarian worship. If this latter is being carried out in a dull, uninspiring and out-dated way, the solution is to take steps to ensure that it is done in a lively inspiring and relevant manner. Rejecting institutional religion altogether is tantamount to turning one's back on a societal expression of one's religious faith and that is harmful.

Besides, such an attitude implicitly denies any social dimension to religion. This is equivalent to saying that religion should not seek the betterment of society, should not challenge unjust structures, is totally impervious to the various ways in which humans concretely live out their day-to-day lives on earth. This would make religion a disembodied, inhuman, ethereal and other-worldly thing-a religion that would be more fitted for angelic spirits. This kind of religion would end up being even more irrelevant and meaningless than the caricature it sought to avoid!

Popular Idols

The age of idolatry is far from over. And the biggest offenders in this area are, sadly enough, religious believers of all persuasions. Many sincerely good and pious people gradually end up in worshipping a "god" of their own fabrication. The advantage of such "idolatry" should be obvious: a "god" tailored to our own specifications is easy to get along with. Such a "god", made in our own image and likeness, will not challenge or disturb our pet prejudices and vices. As Voltaire tellingly remarked, "If God made us in his image, we have certainly returned the compliment." By no means is this always done "with full knowledge and full consent": most people do this unconsciously. Such deviance must be ruthlessly shown up for what it is-so that we can get on with the real job of encountering God in all authenticity and learn to obey in faith his discomfiting call as well as listen to his unpopular words! A few popular "idols" are listed below. Let us not forgets that each of them succeeds as a popular idol only because it starts off with an important theological truth and then exaggerates it. Remember, an error is an exaggerated truth!

The "Aspirin" God: The name here is derived from the current popular anti-headache-pill: aspro, ancin, crocin or whatever (I have used the more generic term, "aspirin"). Such "mental analgesics"-the contemporary "opium of the people") are useful, nay indispensable, constituents of everyone's medicine chest. It is most sensible to stock a few such "soothers": who knows when the next hangover or headache will present itself? In which case, we dose ourselves with the appropriate amount and then promptly forget about them till the next crisis. And, for many people, God is just like that. He exists:

he's "there", all right-just like those wonderful tablets. And whenever they have a "spiritual" problem, they dose themselves with God (a novena prayer or a hurried visit to the nearest shrine) and proceed to forget about his existence until the next hassle comes along. And, of course, we should turn to God, as to a reliable friend, for strength and inspiration, any time we have to face one of life's upsets-but surely not *only* at such times! Indeed, a Relationship which is based exclusively on such moments, where demands for immediate help are expected to be fulfilled to the letter and without delay, would be a pale, childish and slender one indeed. Could this be the main reason why, for many people, their prayer-life remains so stagnant and shallow? Doesn't the prayer of such people boil down to a mere shopping list presented to a "super-market" god? And if the Establishment doesn't render prompt and efficient service, don't they campaign to boycott the Store?

The "Puppeteer" God: This is the deity of all – clergy and laity! – who champion a naive, uncritical understanding of God's way with us. They understand common religious phrases like "God's Will" to mean that God has pre-determined, prearranged and pre-programmed every detail of our lives, right up to, and including pre-fixing the exact date, time and place of our death. And, indeed, such people often manage to derive some kind of consolation in times of crisis from such a world-view. They say, "Well, God knows best. He made this happen so it must be for our overall good." But in doing so, they have solved one problem (the scandal of the suffering of the innocent) by creating another (implying that we are not really free at all). For, if it is God who's been pulling the strings all along, in effect, then shouldn't we logically blame him for the gang-rape of the sole, helpless woman or the latest instance of child-abuse? Why didn't he work out things such that decent, innocent people don't have to go through such traumatic – and often fatal – experiences? Now, it is true that most religious do teach some kind of divine providence. But, unless I am sadly mistaken, these also teach human freedom, yet their understanding of divine providence thus makes the former an empty word! Indeed, religion and morality and all their associated language of praise and blame, sin and grace, redemption and salvation, would have little meaning were there no such thing as authentic human freedom!

This is no place to elaborate a harmony of providence and freedom.[35] Suffice is it to say, here, that one should be wary of popular and uncritical statements about divine providence that make a mockery of the fact that we are really free, Freud and Skinner notwithstanding.

The "Policeman" God: This is the kind of god upheld by that character in Dostoyevsky's *The Brothers Karamazov* who said, "If God did not exist, everything would be permitted." In other words, his "god" was required to prop up the moral order: were there no "god", there'd be no moral laws, no ethical "do's and don'ts" and one could act as he or she pleased, with impunity. Implicit to this understanding is that certain actions are morally evil because "god" arbitrarily decided to make them so. The "god" presupposed is one who, having nothing better to do one day, decided to create a moral code for his person-creatures-and, being the spoilsport and stick-in-the-mud that he was (no one would put it quite so bluntly, perhaps, but this is what it actually means), he chose the most boring and dullest things and stipulated that they would be virtuous acts and then picked up the most exciting and interesting ventures and declared them to be sinful. Naturally, the most spontaneous and human reaction to such fascistic impositions would be rebellion, but for the fact that-with admirable divine foresight-that too is forbidden and sinful! This, in effect, is the god of the legalist, the Pharisee and the fanatic, self-appointed Regents of the Most High, zealous to wreak terrible vengeance for the least infringement of the divine code, even on the most unintentional, well-meaning and unwary transgressor. And soon a whole accumulation of accompanying rubrics and norms – the expression of ignorance and threatened male chauvinism for the most part – grows tip alongside. In the end we are left with such a legal labyrinth that only specially trained members of the exclusive Club can interpret. But, we needs must ask, is something evil just

---

35 I have attempted this in my notes Cyril Desbruslais. 1985. *The Philosophy of God*, Pune, Jnana-Deepa Vidyapeeth, pp. 51-60 (mimeographed notes). This Notes will soon be published.

because it is forbidden by God, or does God forbid it because it is evil? Is not an action evil for a human because it would totally frustrate the human growth of that person-whose very humanness is founded on the creative will of God? And if the only reason why I don't run riot all over town, raping, looting and killing is that I live in fear of God taking punitive action against me at some future date ... isn't that a rather retarded moral consciousness? Shouldn't a mature adult be capable of seeing the inherent evil of rape-how it dishonours and dehumanises both victim and aggressor – without requiring a divine condemnation to restrain him from such ventures? And have we not met people of sterling moral character and selfless commitment who do not believe in God and have no need for a religious prop for their ethical conduct? After all, lollipops and rewards are necessary to make a little child behave. But when a fully grown man or woman will only "be good" if promised a reward (heaven) or threatened with a punishment (hell), something is assuredly not quite in order!

Not that the fact of God's unconditional love necessitates that he regard us indifferently, with a beatific and stupid smile, whether we do good or bad. The image of an "all-loving" deity who remains unmoved at the sight of his elder, stronger son (whom he loves) bullying his younger, weaker daughter (whom he also loves) is as repugnant as it is blatantly false. God's love is unconditional: he loves both victim and aggressor and this does not preclude his showing his love for the victim by care and his love for the aggressor by anger. Anger is not incompatible with love and it certainly is possible to "be angry and sin not"! (Eph 4:26) This should not be taken to imply that I agree with those who hold that natural calamities, diseases and other misfortunes are the ways God punishes the unjust and the impious. A cursory glance at the world around us would reveal that it is the poor, the innocent and the weak who most often have to face these harrowing experiences! Once again, I refer the reader to my notes on the *Philosophy of God*,[36] where I mention – *inter alia* – that God's punishment of the oppressor is expressed rather through his raising up of prophetic voices to denounce injustice as also to disturb the guilty party's peace of mud by the pricking of his conscience!

36 *Op. cit.*

One could prolong this catalogue of idols. There is, besides, the dhobi god: the one the believer uses to get his "soul" purified of sin by routine rituals (confessions or purificatory baths). As a result, one takes moral endeavour very lightly-just as one is not too careful to keep his nice white shirt clean, knowing that he has an excellent laundryman at his beck and call. Indeed, God is more willing to forgive us our faults than we are even willing to ask, but a more mature level of morality is required to ensure that this doesn't end up in making a laughing stock of religiously-grounded moral behaviour.[37] Then there is the racist "god": the gad that assures me that only I, and those few others whose religious views coincide exactly with mine, will be saved. The rest, a veritable *massa damnata* (Latin: damned mass), would be consigned to eternal perdition, no matter how upright or committed their lives may be! Such views are perhaps the result of misunderstanding of the scriptural notion of "election", cf being part of a "chosen people". Closer examination of the relevant texts will no doubt reveal that such "divine choice" does not imply any rejection of all others: just the opposite! The "election" is but a being set aside to let everyone know of God's particular love for the poor or that God loves everyone, unconditionally. There is no connotation of exclusive privileges or prerogatives!

Atheism's Critique

Paul Ricoeur dubbed the trio Nietzsche-Marx-Freud "Masters of Suspicion" for they, in effect cautioned us against being hasty and naive in our claims to have had mystical experiences. Often times, when we thought we were encountering God, they tell us, we were actually being confronted by unhealthy aspects of ourselves. Of course, in their view, all religious experience is only that and nothing more: there never is any real encounter with the supernatural for there is no such entity. My position is that their interpretation is, after all, too reductionist. A good deal of what commonly passes off as coming face-to-face with God *is* a mistaken revelling in an unhealthy aspect of ourselves. But not all reports of religious experience can be dismissed in that way!

---

37 See the next chapter.

As the research of scholars like William James (a professional psychologist) and Henri Bergson (a professional philosopher) have shown us, in every religion, in every culture and at every period of history, there have been-and continue to be-great mystics. Now, not all of these can be written off as cranks, social misfits who-consciously or not-fabricate their mystical flights out of their own inadequacies and seek to live off their escapist convictions. Many mystics were undoubtedly eminent persons of obvious psychological maturity: radical reformers, they challenged the existing social and religious mores of their times and were frequently prosecuted by the powers that be, sacred and secular. They were men and women of personality and vision, who were inspiring leaders and gifted administrators. They were able to launch revolutionary movements and attract charismatic followers for pioneering ventures. Their writings stir us today. In short, they emerge at leastas psychologically sound as the best of us-if not more so! Their mystical writings can't be put on the same level as that of the hysterical old lady next door. Not all religious experiences pale and wilt before the ruthless assault of philosophical "suspicion".

But some do. And it is surely worth our while to hearken to the caveats of Nietzsche, Marx and Freud. J. P. Stern summed up their perennial insights so well:

> They saw their undertaking as the solving of a secret and all opposition to it as a conspiracy: a conspiracy of men with vested social interests, thought Marx; of men with vested moral and religious interests, thought Freud; of men who choose to be only half alive and resent the few who live generously and dangerously thought Nietzsche.[38]

Marx: According to the father of all leftist thinkers, "religion is the opium of the people": everybody knows he said that. But what many people do not know is that, according to him, it is not the oppressors who dose the oppressed with that convenient analgesic! On the contrary, religion is a drug administered to the oppressed *by themselves* so as to make their painful lot more bearable. Now

38 J. P. Stern. 1979. *Nietzsche*, Glasgow, Fontana/Collins, p. 13.

there's nothing wrong in taking a painkiller as a temporary measure or when the source of one's agony is irremovable. But it is foolish to take a pain-killer when one can remove its source once and for all. And Marx's observation is most legitimately directed against those victims of social injustice who, instead of rising up to challenge their oppressors and demand their rights, resign themselves to their misery and wait patiently for their compensatory slice of "pie in the sky when they die". Now, where this is the case, we cannot but wholeheartedly endorse the Marxian critique, collaborate to extirpate this phony religious sense and conscientise the people to concerted action for justice. And authentic religion can, far from being an opium of the people, prove itself a catalyst for social action, as the champions of a theology (or philosophy) of liberation do.

Nietzsche: It is all too easy to dismiss his strident rantings against God as sterile ravings of a deranged neurotic which, admittedly, is how he ended his days. But, behind all his pitiful arrogance and schizophrenic posturing there is a terrible charge that still rings true: religion has proved for a good many to be but a disguise for, and a justification of, mediocrity. There has been an all too hasty canonisation of virtues like resignation, humility and meekness, without a counter-balancing emphasis on initiative, courage and self-assertion. Too long have we viewed these last as manifestations of proud independence and vicious ambition. But there is a positive independence and ambition: all these are susceptible to a liberative interpretation and this has been inexcusably overlooked. We have a responsibility for self-realisation and a little mature reflection will enable us to recognise that it is only isolated self-seeking, without any social sensitivity, divorced from all inter-personal relations, is self-destructive. Hence, any quest to fulfil one's dreams, ambitions and healthy independence which makes use of cheating, bribery and other unjust means will assuredly not make one more fully human, more fully alive and so must be rejected. But seen in a proper perspective and pursued with a proper orientation, ambition and "aiming high" are all essential means to attain our total human liberation, ensuring the full flowering of our dynamic potentials. Nietzsche does well to remind us of all this. On the other hand, a blind and disproportionate endorsement of those allegedly "manly" virtues, without situating them in their proper humanising context can only lead to the worst justifications of racism, colonialism and oppression. Hitler and Ayn Rand are illustrative examples!

Freud: He suggests that religion could be a cover-up for childhood regression: a religious believer, in effect, is one who is afraid to grow up and accept responsibility for his/her own life. Instead, there is a projection of the childhood "big daddy" God to whom one can run to get all problems solved, rather than face up to challenges oneself. Of course "running to Daddy" was all right in one's infancy and childhood: to need to do this in adolescence and adulthood was sheer cowardice and irresponsibility. Religion, thus, for Freud, is based on illusion-which is not the same as delusion. The latter is plainly false. What characterises the former is wish-fulfilment – the kind of *deus ex machina,* wish-fulfilment, that is a regular solution for trashy movies and cheap cliff-hangers. Of course, when and where this is the case, we cannot but campaign with the Austrian sage for the eradication of such gods. But this is not always the case, whenever religious experience and practices are discovered. As we pointed out earlier, James and Bergson, assure us that some very psychologically well-adjusted types, outstanding in administration, leadership and radical thinking, have been religious. They would be able to teach Freud and his ilk a thing or two

Some Christian Responses

The challenging criticisms of the "Masters of Suspicion" – whose words may be viewed as the paradigm of all serious attacks of depth made against religion in theory and practice-did not fall everywhere on deaf ears. Where once upon a time, such atheistic criticisms were met with harsh anathema, believers were prepared to listen and dialogue. Vatican II was one such instance, at the official, institutional level. But there were many individual Christians who, in their private capacity, responded to the charge and learnt thereby how to purify their understanding of God and, consequently, deepen their religious convictions. People of other faiths would do well to emulate them. We now consider three representative responses: two are Protestants, one is from a Catholic-more concretely, we listen to a Lutheran pastor, an Anglican Bishop and a Jesuit priest.

Dietrich Bonhoeffer (1909-1945), was a German theologian and member of the outspoken Confessing Church. In 1943 he was arrested by the Nazis for his denunciation of National Socialism and was hanged in 1945. In his controversial Letters and Papers from Prison, edited and published by his friend, Eberhard Bethge, he called for the establishment of a "religionless Christianity", one of his most hotly debated ideas. The traditional "religious a priori" upon which the various faith communities are built, he points out, is an alleged innate sense of hopelessness, helplessness and inadequacy in the human person, which is taken as the sole indispensable path towards God. Nowadays, however, "Man has learned to cope with all questions of importance without recourse to God as a working hypothesis". Nor did he make this statement in disgust, intending it to be a negative comment on the crass perversity of modern man's condemnable irreligiousness: it was rather his recognition of the fact that the modern person had "come of age" and required a new approach to God than the antiquated one of human weakness, helplessness and insufficiency. Just as, in the past, religious leaders had to accommodate themselves to the fact that believers were no longer turning, in ignorance, to God when dealing with issues of health and weather, but to medical science and meteorology and learn to accept that this was not a movement of wicked and perverse human pride, so they would have to recognise that we no longer need to turn to God when faced with the "ultimate questions" (death, guilt, etc.). Indeed, they should give up trying to thrust God and religion on us at moments of emotional and personal crisis, such as the death of a loved one, thereby taking advantage of human frailty. It is a sad fact that most clergy only know how to make God and religion relevant to the human condition when one is in a "limit" situation", when one feels lost, helpless and unable to cope. This kind of approach, says Bonhoeffer, is pointless and ignoble, not to say totally unchristian:

> Pointless, because it looks to me like an attempt to put a grown-up person back into adolescence, i.e. make one dependent on things which, in fact, one is not dependent any more, thrusting one back into the midst of problems which are, in fact, not problems for one anymore. Ignoble,

> because this amounts to an effort to exploit one's weaknesses for purposes that are alien and not freely subscribed to. Unchristen, because for Christ, is being substituted one stage in the religious development of the human person.

Bonheoffer feels it would be far better to teach man to live manfully without answers to the so-called "ultimate questions", rather than use these as a way to break down his last vestiges of courage and self-confidence. There seems to be something basically perverse in an approach that exploits the strategy of falling upon "unhappy people, in their weakest moment (to) force upon them a sort of religious conversion", when they are too broken and dispirited to resist.

So, in place of the long-standing traditionally 'religious' understanding of things, Bonheoffer proposes a more relevant "worldly interpretation" of the human condition. This implies living *etsi Deus non daretur* (as if there were no God-the use of the subjunctive indicates that he most certainly does believe in God). In other words, we must live as if God were not "a working hypothesis" or, as he puts it even more provocatively, "living before God as if there were no God". At the practical level it means believing in God, being aware that one lives in the shadow of his love and strengthening grace ("living before God"), but not expecting miracles and revelations to make one's way any the easier ("as if there were no God"). This is what he thinks authentic Christianity-authentic religion, we might prefer to say-call us to.

John Robinson (1919-1983), the controversial Anglican Bishop of Woolwich, in England, re-stated the questions of his mentor, Bonheoffer, in a slightly more pastoral way: Why must religion persist in trying to make us aware of our need for God, only in terms of our weakness and helplessness, when we are the end of our tether? Why not seek to encounter God in terms of our strength and sufficiency? Is God, in effect, no more than a crutch for a lame man-and irrelevant to a healthy person? Should we not seek God in the very depths of our being, rather than at the uttermost fringes of our finitude? It is in this context that he advocates panentheism the consideration not so much that we are God, but that all things are in God ("in him we live and move and have our being"). But it is in his *The New Reformation* that we come across his most famous and quotable quote: "God is intellectually superfluous, emotionally dispensable and morally intolerable". In other words, he is questioning the traditional and more common "paths" to God that we tend to take. God should not be a kind of intellectual stop-gap: one we regularly trot in to give a nice *deus ex machina* answer to our current baffling questions. This scapegoat "god" is but a convenient cover-up for our ignorance and, very often, quite effectively puts a halt to deeper reflection and research. Besides, as the positive sciences begin to make more and more progress, "god" will be pushed further and further away from the sphere of our ordinary, everyday life! Nor should "god" be brought in as a kind of security blanket, something to cling to in moments of stress and strain. Such a "god" would put an end to more mature, more outreaching means of dealing with such exigencies: getting out of oneself, seeking guidance and support of a more tangible kind. Nor, as we have already seen, should be required to prop up the moral order: if the only reason I "behave" is fear of God's punishment or hope of God's reward, that attests to a very shallow, very immature and very childish moral capacity. The real basis for belief in God should be the fact the we have personally encountered Him. It is out of the love that develops from such a mystical experience that one cannot but have a place for God in one's life; I heed Him because I love Him and not the other way round! This loving relationship is the sole basis of any healthy liberative religious life.

Pierre Teilhard de Chardin SJ (1881-1955), is a valuable counter-blast against Nietzsche, who was convinced that a serious-minded Christian had no choice but to hate the world and the things of this world. This might have been characteristic of much popular Christian piety and spirituality and some such idea, to a greater or lesser extent ,is found in all religions. An admittedly oppressive interpretation of the maya (illusion) theory in Hinduism is most evidently world-negating. However, the eminent Jesuit scientist is a living, proof that not every religious person has such an attitude!. On his own admission, he was "by upbringing and intellectual training" a true "child of heaven", but "by temperament and professional studies" also a "child of the earth". We know full well that Teilhard was something of a pioneering spirit in all this and had to face the threat of censure from feelingless and unsympathetic powers-that-be, but he persevered and his stand has now been fully vindicated by Vatican II. When he was yet a Marxist, Roger Garaudy, in *From Anathema to Dialogue,* remarked that if there were more believers of Teilhard's stamp, there would be no need for the continuance of atheistic humanism.[39] Teilhard's oft-quoted remark to the effect that religion had produced too many lambs and we need some lions for a change is no call for a brand of neo-Nietzcheanism as his detractors would have it, but for a more bold, courageous and assertive Christianity-one worthy of the great explorer-missionaries and the champions of the oppressed.[40]

Concluding Critical Comments

Bonheoffer and Robinson are like a breath of fresh air as they call for a religious faith that takes its roots not in human helplessness and misery-as if God is only relevant for the weak, the sick and the confused. Instead, in a vision redolent of St Irenaeus (c. 140-202), they sound a clarion call to all Christians-and by extension all authentic religious believers-to recognise that "the glory of God is a person fully human, fully alive". For we are made in his image and likeness and are not meant to think of ourselves as sick, ugly and go about demeaning ourselves and grovelling. Of course, as always "there is a danger in going too far"-a common objection of the timid whenever a newer approach is suggested. But let us not forget that we went a bit too far along the lines of the traditional approach, killing so much of human drive and initiative in the name of religion and provoking men like Nietzsche to say what they did. As always, we must be on our guard against exaggeration and losing a sense of proportion: this is attendant on any human venture. Finally, let us not forget that the stress implied in St. Irenaeus' vision is authentically Biblical too and has older roots in Christian tradition, for one.

39 Roger Garaudy. 1967. *From Anathema to Dialogue: The Challenge of Marxist-Christian Cooperation.* London: Collins.

40 William M. Shea 2004. *The Lion and the Lamb Evangelicals and Catholics in America.* Oxford; New York: Oxford University Press. http://site.ebrary.com/id/10103522.

Robinson precises the areas where, in his opinion, we should not too easily turn to God for help in crisis: the intellectual, the emotional and the moral. And there is a certain challenge for all of us in this message. Our faith in God shouldn't provide a brake for scientific endeavour, research and experiment. As for our emotional needs, I think the issue here is a bit more complex. There is a kind of personal, emotional strength in time of need that only God can provide and no human depth of love and friendship can replace. But there is also the need for a certain human, tangible companionship in an hour of crisis (a hand to hold, a voice to be heard and a look of love to be sensed) which normally we cannot claim from God. On occasion, there may be more or less intense mystical moments where we can practically sense God's touch and hear healing words. But, generally speaking, it would seem to be "God's way"-judging how usually things go-that we turn to each other, as fellow-travellers on the way, for that kind of support. The very Christian doctrine of the Incarnation appears to imply that God upholds the principle of subsidiarity: He doesn't want us to turn to him for what we can find, by ourselves, through the help of each other. From God we receive the assurance of total acceptance, total unconditional love-even though He knows through and through, warts and all, as the phrase goes. No human friend and lover can know us so intimately as God does-and yet God finds us lovable. This is an important realisation: how often do we fear that "if people really knew what we were, what we thought privately, would they really love us!" God knows us so and God loves and accepts us. That is a liberative insight, if ever there was one.

But there is one area of insufficiency where God and God alone steps in. For want of a better word, I call that "metaphysical insufficiency": the fact that, as finite, created beings we remain ever totally ontologically dependent on him, unlike the table, which is only partially dependent on the carpenter. It required his assistance only for its assemblage: its raw materials were previously existing independent of him and, after he's put the whole thing together, it can carry on existing without his help-can even "outlive" him! Not so with us. We are dependent on God, not only for "our assemblage" (which he takes care of, with the help of human and other collaborators-the principle of subsidiarity, again), but also for our "raw materials" and-most important-for our "staying in existence". The nearest parallel to conservation-our here and now dependence on God for "staying in existence"-is the light bulb and its dependence on the power station for it to stay lit. Only God can provide for our metaphysical insufficiency.

One final word. Why is it that we tend to become aware of our need for God only in a "limit situation", when we are "the end of our tether" as Bonheoffer lamented. This is, after all, quite understandable-not that I'm trying to justify a regression to that worm-theology that Nietzsche so much deplored! God, after all, is as necessary to us as air (even more than that, but let's not be too pedantic). Is it surprising, then, that we tend to take both God and air for granted? We know that we need air to survive, yet are hardly-if ever-aware of the fact that we live and move and have our being in it ... until its supply begins to be cut off: in such a "limit situation" we realise how necessary it was to us. Now, precisely because God is so essential to our existence, we don't notice his presence and action in us until, in a limit situation we are at the end of our tether! Let us not forget that Bonheoffer's most illuminating' and powerful insights came to him when he was in a "limit" situation: in prison, with a sentence of death just around the corner!

Some Quotes

"Men will wrangle for religion; write for it; fight for it; anything but - live for it."

– Charles Colton

"We have just enough religion to make us hate, but not enough to make us love on another."

– Jonathan Swift

"Religion that is pure and undefiled before God and the Father is this: to care for orphans and widows in their affliction and to keep oneself unstained by the world."

– James 1:27

Chapter 7

INSTITUTIONALISED RELIGION

Introduction

We have already had occasion to recognise that, for many people, religion has been perceived as more a hindrance than a help towards a genuine encounter with God. Common enough slogans among the young today are one's like "Jesus: Yes! The Church: No!" or, in its more general formula,"1 believe in God, but not in religion!"

Yet, as we have seen, some kind of institutionalisation of religion is more or less inevitable-unless we are content to reduce it to some kind of private, exclusively "spiritual" preoccupation. In fact, we can cite at least three major reasons why religious experience must, sooner or later, be given some kind of form and structure. First, inasmuch as we are embodied beings, anything that is left in its purely intangible and disembodied state, cannot but touch us lightly and leave us with an over-riding sense of dissatisfaction: if we wish to take it seriously, we must lend it tangibility and embodiedness through some kind of institutionalisation. Secondly, if religion is to have some social significance, if it is to have some transformative impact upon society-inspiring people to action for justice and in support of the eco-system-it requires some kind of communitarian expression. Finally, if it is not to be some fleeting, fly-by-night kind of thing, here today and gone tomorrow, coming to birth and dying along with each isolated individual's alleged encounter with the powers that be, it must needs have some concrete form to ensure the sharing, preservation and development of the tradition.

This does not mean that I am giving whole-hearted endorsement to each and every dimension of the concrete organised religions of today. Our "oppressive-liberative" yardstick must be employed here ruthlessly, too. And our scrutiny should be primarily directed at the understanding of religious leadership and guidance, for it is these men (the gender-slanted term is utilised very deliberately) who invariably emerge as the exclusive custodians of religious institutionalisation. And call them what you will – priests, pastors, pujaris, imams, shamans, bonzes, rabbis, witch-doctors or whatnot – much of what is quite justly condemned in organised religion is the fault of certain unscrupulous and oppressive individuals of this motley crew, whose arrogant claims and despotic behaviour are the main cause for the disgust of many people for organised religion in general and its officials in particular.

Priestly and Prophetic Leaders

Religious leaders, for practical purposes, may be sub-divided into two main types: the priestly and the prophetic. The former are characterised by the fact that they have a cult to perform, the latter by the commission that they have a word to speak. The notion is not very precise and clear: it's often a question of emphasis and a matter of situating a particular religious official more at one end of the spectrum than the other.

The Priest, in the history of religions, is a cultic figure: his role being to ensure the proper and prescribed way of honouring and worshipping the divinity. One became a priest either by being the male offspring of some priestly caste (Brahmins) or tribe (Levi) or by the ceremony of ordination. The priest was seen originally as the great mediator between the all-holy God and the all-sinful human. He was, ideally, pontifex maximus – the great Bridge over the awful gulf. The main function of the priest, according to the traditional formula was "to take humans to God, to bring God to us". None but these specially set apart beings could dare to fulfil this indispensable role of mediation. None but they knew how to do the job: what precise words to pronounce and which particular rubrics to perform. No "mere" lay-person was considered worthy to pray: the priest was the only efficacious intermediary who'd assure blessings on oneself and one's loved ones, curses on one's enemies, atonement sacrifices for one's sins ... and all at a fee, of course. Furthermore, no doubt in order to ensure there'd be no blasphemous usurping of his power by lesser mortals, the rules governing valid rituals became more and more elaborate-and meticulous exactitude was demanded, else the whole process would be rendered invalid-and the language used was invariably some extinct, recondite "sacred" language-in which alone prayers were to be couched-the study of which was restricted, often at pain of death, to the clerical coteries. In the end, the priest emerged as more powerful than God: he knew which words and gestures would oblige the moody and susceptible divinity to do his bidding. It is not too difficult to see how men of such ilk would slide to the oppressive end of the spectrum.

The Prophet (literally a spokesperson) has not so much a rubric to perform as a word to proclaim. The prophet can be of any sex or community. Whereas the priest's role is more usually conceived as getting the supernatural powers that be to do as he directs, the prophet's function is just the opposite: to interpret God's word and thence direct the people to action. Prophetic figures are recognisable in all religions-and from out of them, too: Karl Marx and Che Guevera, to name but two, were not even religious believers. But if the great prophets have ever summoned people to action for justice and liberation, there have also been "false" prophets: time-serving demagogues who would enlist their oratory in favour of the status quo, religious and secular. There have been "prophets" like Hitler, who "interpreting the signs of the times" have sent their people forth on a mission of pogrom and riot. Let us not under-estimate the creative power of human beings. We have an uncanny ability to distort or reorient the noblest of things for shoddy and unsavoury purposes!

Hierarchy and Democracy

Accountability is the only way to check a gradual slide towards despotism and fascism. If absolute power corrupts absolutely, unaccountable religious power can lead to the worst from of absolute corruption. This is because religious authority claims jurisdiction over even our hidden thoughts and aspirations and because religious authority, more often than not, maintains that it is answerable to God alone and is not obliged to take the views of the people into account. The common folk invariably have no say as to just who would be their religious leader and the extent to which the latter would seek and listen to their reactions is almost totally at the mercy of his whims and fancies. Very often religious leaders read the slightest questioning as a manifestation of rebellion, disobedience and move in fast to stem what they understand as the beginnings of a dangerous new heresy. As Leonardo Boff puts it in his controversial book, *The Church: Charism and Power*,[41] it's not that Church leaders are inherently bad, it's the Church structures which are: the undemocratic set-up, where the people are not required to give their vote for anything and don't have to be consulted on any matter (unless the goodness of the local leader permits it): this is what makes hierarchies oppressive. That there must be some kind of hierarchy and leadership goes without saying. But when those in power are submitted to a structure which isolates them from the people and gives them the impression (which soon hardens into an attitude) that the views of the latter are of little or no consequence ... all this effectively-paves the way to a "lording-it-over-the-flock" mentality that is the basis of clerical and religious oppression. By an accident of history, most religions emerged at a time when absolute monarchy was the only viable socio-political structure and so it was naively assumed that it was divine will that any form of religious institutionalism should automatically assume this format. Consequently, most religious authorities look askance at any talk of democracy and the rights of human persons.

---

41 Leonardo Boff. 1985. *Church, Charism and Power: Liberation Theology and the Institutional Church*. New York: Crossroad.

And in Christianity ...

It is significant that the early Christian community never felt constrained to borrow models or titles of authority from prevailing religious offices-and there was an abundance of such to emulate. They preferred to appropriate nomenclature from secular and civil life: *diakonos* (deacon, literally, a server at table, a waiter), *episkopos* (whence our bishop, literally an overseer presbyter – an elder) and so on. The Greek word for priest, *hiereus*, is never used as the title of any Christian official or leader. It was only referred to members of the Jewish or pagan priesthoods and, in the letter to the Hebrews, to Jesus, our one eternal high priest (we'll discuss this in a moment). Indeed, the Old Testament doesn't even see the priesthood as a vocation: one is a priest simply because one belongs to the (priestly) tribe of Levi. All the oft-quoted "vocation" texts (ig, 6:1-10, Jer 1:1-10 etc) concern the vocation of the prophet, who can be from any tribe or community, even of the feminine sex. And, once again, *prophetes* (literally, a spokes-person, one who is authorised to speak on another's behalf), like *apostolos* (emissary) are titles of secular officials. Even the place where the community used to meet for prayer and the breaking of the bread (when it became a special building set aside for that purpose and no longer the house of some wealthy, generous Christian-usually a woman) was called by the common name of assembly hall or *ekklesia* (literally a convocation or place where people were called together). It was not hailed as a temple (naos), shrine or "house of God". Indeed, the only temple (naos) in the Christian dispensation is the human body, the "temple of the Holy Spirit" (I Cor. 6:19 ff). It was much later, when the slide towards "spiritualisation" had set in that there began to be talk of Christian priests and "churches" (from the Greek *kyriakos*, dominical, house of the Lord).

It is good to remind ourselves that Jesus was not a priest but a layman. He was a Jew who did not come from the tribe of Levi and stands out as the prophet par excellence. *Hebrews* does see him as our "one eternal High priest" (8:1, 10:21 ff) but precisely to emphasise how Jesus' mediatorship has made all priesthoods redundant. He "once and for all" brought God to humans and humans to God: no longer do we require an ordained Pontifex, or Bridger of the gap. At

Jesus' death, the temple curtain was torn in two (Mt 27:51): now everyone has access to the sanctuary. *Hebrews*, of course, speaks analogically of Jesus' "ordination" at Calvary, but let us not forget that this was a secular, political event, not a religious ceremony! Jesus was not crucified on an altar between two candlesticks but on a hill outside the walls of the Holy City, on what was the rubbish dump, amid two terrorists, at the crossroads leading to the City, a place where people met to argue, haggle and exchange ribald jokes.

The real "office" which we Christian "priests" (a contradiction in terms if ever there was one) exercise is that of prophet – a real vocation, modelled on the life and mission of Jesus. Ours is not a cult to be preformed with rubrical exactitude, but a Word (God's unpopular Word) that must be spoken. The liturgy and the sacraments are not so much cultic acts aimed at influencing a bad-tempered and susceptible divinity, but a prophetic word that empowers and "sends forth" God's people on a mission to build the kingdom. Nor does this give us any "power" that is denied to the "mere lay person" as we shall see next.

Two Kinds of Identity

There are two common approaches to establish one's identity. I call them *identity-by-exclusion* and *identity-by-inclusion*. Normally, whenever a person or a group"?-persons has what is known as an identity-crisis", the problem is sought to be solved by listing what that person or group, alone, can do, setting them apart from the rest of mortals. This, I think, is a very immature way of defining oneself: in terms of some exclusive power or privilege which devolves upon one, cutting him off from others. And this has been the traditional way in which the Christian priest-particularly the Catholic priest-has understood himself: his "ordination" has given him certain powers (e.g. to "forgive sins", effect the transubstantiation at Mass, etc.) that no lay person can have or assume. The list was much longer once upon a time. But, gradually, lay people are being granted a share in many activities and ministries that were once considered the sacrosanct reserve of the priest alone (as Eucharistic ministers, lectors and so on): no wonder the Catholic priest began to have a "crisis of identity", and consequently, there was a decline of vocations.

Perhaps the best way for me to explain what I mean by "identity-by-inclusion" is through the example of the soldier. All citizens of a country-both civilians as much as members of the armed forces-are expected to love their motherland and, to the best of their ability, defend it against the depredations of an unjust aggressor. But this is a responsibility of vital importance and it is necessary that at least some citizens devote the time and energy to undergo the rigorous training and discipline that would ensure the job be done most effectively. Thus, a few of us, either as the result of a kind of inner urge ("vocation"), or thanks to some careful canvassing ("vocation promotion"), present ourselves as candidates for the army, navy or air force. Those who finally "make it" to the marching out parade, commissioning or whatever, do not, thereby, receive any special powers or privileges in the normal sense of the term, that are denied to the "man in civvy street."[42] It's just that they have been more thoroughly prepared to fulfil a serious responsibility, in a manner more effective, than an average, untrained person would be able to do. The only "difference" between a trained soldier and the man in the street is that the former will make a more capable defender of his country than the latter. It is along lines such as these that I understand the "identity" of the priest.

All Christians are called, by virtue of their baptism to prophetically speak God's unpopular word to a recalcitrant world. All are called to bear witness to the presence of the Risen Lord who calls us to commit ourselves to the building up of the Kingdom of Justice, Love and Peace "on earth as it is in heaven". All of us are gifted with the discerning power of the Holy Spirit so as to "read the signs of the times" and figure out how to respond to God's summons within the existential set-up of today. A few of us have been "set aside" and given a special training in the Scriptures, in Philosophy, Theology, Spirituality pastoral skills to ensure that the job is properly done-by priest and lay person alike. The priest's identity, then, does not consist in his having particular privileges and powers that are denied to the "non-priest" but in his being specifically equipped to ensure

42 The ordinary "civilians" or persons, who are not used to a luxurious, elite life-style.

that the very important task of "keeping alive our response to the Christ event" (phrase it as you will) be effectively maintained down the ages.

Let's come back to our traditional, identity-crisis-ridden Catholic priest. He looks with dismay at his erstwhile long list of exclusive privileges, prerogatives and powers and finds that they have now shrunk to just two: celebrating the Eucharist (more precisely, pronouncing the "transubstantiating words" of the Consecration) and "hearing confessions". No wonder his identity is in crisis! After all, now that married men-and even women!-have begun to claim access to his exclusive prerogatives, what is left to distinguish him from family men (and women)? But, perhaps his fears would be allayed, were he to look at his identity in terms of sharing with everyone the same responsibility and dignity: it's just that he, like the soldier, has been able to devote himself full-time to a more rigorous training and discipline to ensure that this task be fulfilled well-by himself and others. And why should he fear if "mere laypeople" shouldered part of the burden? The important thing is that this noble mission be carried out, not by whom it is done. Besides, any identity that is founded on exclusive powers, privileges and prerogatives, will, by that same token soon become oppressive. For it will resent any attempt at feed-back, any democratic-sounding innovations as a revolt against one's sacrosanct and exclusive position. It's difficult to convince someone who has an identity by exclusion that he should be held accountable to others or that they have some say in his appointment or his tenure in a particular post.

Thanks to the vagaries of history – not any divine plan – the office of Christian prophet has ended up by being designated as "priest", perhaps a corruption of presbyter, no doubt in a shift dating from the Byzantine era, where the imperial court was taken as the model for Christian administrative structures. It was also about this time that the assembly hall or secular *ekklesia* was transmuted into the *kyriakos*,[43] from which our English church is derived. There has been a sad over-spiritualisation of the vision and mission of Jesus. To be sure he was no mere political liberator or social reformer (as some,

43 From the Greek, *Kyrios*. Lord or Master – hence, "house of the Lord God".

at the opposite end of the spectrum have tried to demonstrate). He realised that "man does not live by bread alone"[44] or, as even Che Guevera was to acknowledge, "man is not just a stomach: he also hungers for dignity". Jesus was concerned about the whole person, not just our so-called "spiritual" needs. After nourishing the people on the Word of God, he reminded the Apostles that they should take care of the physical hunger of the people as well. He healed people of all manner of diseases and ailments and, according to John, his first "sign" was to convert water into an abundance of wine at a wedding feast. Even if we were to contest, as some do, the historicity of the event, its "sign-value" assuredly points to the importance of the secular, human order. Nor can the recognition that we don't live on "bread alone" imply that we don't need bread at all!

We can't simply turn back the clock. Those of us who are called priests can't just dump the name: a whole network of structures is tied up with that usage and it won't be easy to uproot all of them! We'd do better to rethink our "function" and act accordingly: our job is not so much a cultic preoccupation of seeking, by attention to rubrical exactitude, to make a grumpy deity co-operate with human whims, but to proclaim God's unpopular word to His people (which includes ourselves), making this word "come alive" through our presiding over liturgies and ministering the sacraments: these latter are not cultic actions to be done but prophetic words to be spoken. And the basic message of these words-in continuity with the prophetic utterances from Old Testament times, past the prophetic words of Jesus to the prophetic voices of the Gandhis and Romeros of today-is the same: "Go and set my people free!" This is also called working to build up God's Kingdom on earth. And we must learn to listen to the so-called "laity", for they also share in our prophetic vocation and God speaks to the Church through them, too.

Love Meets Wisdom

This is the title of a significant study of the dialogue between Buddhism and Christianity initiated by the eminent Sri Lankan scholar, Aloysius Pieris SJ. He draws attention to the simplistic

44 Mt 4:4.

polarisations of "agapeic" and "gnostic" religions. The former – like Christianity – speak of salvation through active love and the latter – such as Buddhism – stress wisdom or enlightenment.[45] But, as Pieris points out, this cannot be an "either-or" distinction.

> Gnosis is salvific knowledge and agape is redemptive love. They are certainly not soteriological alternatives, or optional paths to human liberation. They are two mystical moods that can alternate according to the spiritual fluctuations of individuals, groups, and even of entire cultures, without either of them allowing itself to be totally submerged by the other. Nor can they mix to form a hybrid or a "synthesis," for "the twain shall never meet", as Kipling would insist. They are, in other words, two irreducibly distinct languages of the spirit, each incapable, unless aided and complemented by the other, of mediating and adequately expressing the human encounter with the ultimate. Any valid spirituality, Christian or otherwise, must and, as history shows, does retain both poles of religious experience. It is the dialectical interplay of wisdom and love that ensures a progressive movement in the realm of the human spirit.[46]

Love and Wisdom must meet. For without wisdom or enlightenment, love can easily degenerate into fanaticism and wisdom without love can become proud elitism. It is all to easy for one tradition to misrepresent the other with an inexcusable *reductio ad absurdum* and, as Pieris reminds us, there is quite an honour roll of luminaries, of "great generalizers" who have encouraged such a naive approach: "Teilhard de Chardin, S. Radhakrishnan, Carl Gustav Jung, and even the otherwise cautious R. C. Zaehner".

The word Gnosticism is a bad word for Western Christianity: it carries the implications of overweening pride in human capacities, a rejection of any kind of grace or divine help in the human quest for the absolute. Fór, as once again it is Pieris who reminds us, Gnosticism

---

45 Aloysius Pieris. 1988. *Love Meets Wisdom: A Christian Experience of Buddhism, Faith Meets Faith*. Maryknoll, N.Y.: Orbis Books.

46 *Ibid.*, pp. 9-10.

has only been known to European Christianity in one of its heretical variants, Docetism, Manicheism, Catharism, Albigensianism ... But true gnosis is "the liberating knowledge of the Saving Truth dawning on a person already disposed toward its reception by a process of self-purification or renunciation". That is why Pieris will say, in effect, that Christianity must let itself be first evangelised by authentic non-Christian gnosis, before it can preach to them of God's preferential love for the poor.

Maybe we can also learn something from the three traditional *margas* or paths to salvation, spoken of in Hinduism – except that, perhaps, they need to be taken not in some kind of chronological order or position of importance, but in tandem, with one or other pre-dominating at different moments. Every religious movement must practice the path of *karma*, *bhakti* and *jnana*. One must purify one's knowledge and understanding of God (the moment of *jnana*), so as to be motivated hot by legalism or fear of punishment but by devotion and love *(bhakta)* and this, eventually, must issue forth in concrete action for justice (*karma*). Put like that, it does sound very chronological. However, at no one moment can any be divorced from the other two, or some deviation will result. Nor am I merely reproducing the Hindu understanding of these moods for, in classical (and much of traditional) Hinduism, *karma* does not mean action for justice, but ritual action, *yajna* - sacrificial cult done to placate the powers that be - and, besides, jnana is seen as the noblest way, with the other two as qualifying for the beginner who has yet a long way to go.

Rite and Superstition

Religious rites provide a fertile hunting ground for priestcraft and many a hapless and naive victim among the laity has fallen into the clutches of unscrupulous clerics in this area. For the dividing line between devotions (the plural is intentional) and superstition is a very fine one indeed.

The prefix super-suggests that something is overdone or excessive. In superstition, basically, one places exaggerated faith in the capacities of someone or something: in effect, superstition is tantamount to blasphemy for it invests the creature with the unique qualities of the

Creator. One assumes that the performance of a particular act (which could also include the mouthing of certain words or formulae) would oblige the deity to accede to one's wishes. It is in this context that we must beware of all talk of "miraculous" statues or sites (is the divine, healing power tied to an object or a place?). Thus we hear certain clerics claim that the particular statue in their church is "authentic" because it "actually touched" the original-as if it was thereby able to encapsulate some divine attribute. Sadly enough, behind such assertions lurks the unspoken insinuation, "So, put your donation in my coffers, not in that of our arch-rival elsewhere".

What makes certain practices superstitious is not the action itself, but the attitude with which it is performed. For the same action, identically performed by two different persons could be an expression of sincere devotion for one and an activity of gross superstition for the other-it all depends on their dispositions.

The basic question to be asked, couched in the approach of Paul Ricoeur, would be, "Does my action express a 'symbolic' approach to reality or an 'idolic' one?"[47] Both a symbol and an idol claim to "somehow make present" that which they stand for; the basic difference is how they do it-the symbol by "evocation" and the idol by "encapsulation. It is on this latter that superstition takes its root.

The symbol "makes present" that which it symbolises by "calling forth" (e-vocation) the latter, primarily because it participates or shares in some quality of the svmbolizandum. Thus, a dove – not a vulture – can symbolise peace for the dove "participates" or shares in some of the characteristic qualities of peace: gentleness, calmness and the like. However, the symbol, by nature, doesn't pretend to "embody" the symbolizandum. It makes it present but enables us to get in touch with it through the tips of our fingers, as it were: there's much more to peace than a dove, though, by contemplating a dove we can sense peace descending all around us. The idol, on the other hand, makes no such modest claims: it purports to have encapsulated

47 See Kuruvilla Pandikattu. 1999. *Idols to Die, Symbols to Live: Dynamic Interaction between Language, Reality and the Divine.* Intercultural Publications, New Delhi.

what it points to within its slender confines. The divinity is entrapped within the idol, it is contained in it.

Thus a statue can function as an idol or as a symbol: it all depends on the attitude one brings to it. If it is viewed, something like a photograph, as that which helps jog the memory and give us something tangible to stand for the absent and intangible, while making no claims to have locked it up in itself, no problem. But if the statue is alleged to have somehow ensnared within itself the divinity or some of its miraculous powers, then that is idolatry pure and simple. Showing reverence or respect to a statue need not be, in itself, idolatry-any more than my kissing a photograph of my dead mother would be! If my lighting a candle in front of an image of the Virgin is a simple mark of respect, just as I may light a lamp or an *agarbatti* before a portrait of my dead parents, then this is not idolatry. However, if I believe that the statue has power to grant my petition or bring about some miraculous healing by itself, then this is superstition, or "over-standing", that is, taking a stand too much in the fancied powers and virtues of a man-made thing, attributing to it an efficacy which God alone can have. Putting it briefly, a symbol merely apprehends (etymologically, just touches), an idol comprehends (encapsulates).

The biblical injunction on the making of images is, no doubt, linked with God recognising in the human person his own image and likeness (Gen 1:26). Since the human person is God's image and likeness, there is no need to try and improve on that with other creations. Yet, it should be evident that there is no ban on the making of statues (or taking of photographs or painting landscapes, all of which-to be logical-would stand equally prohibited) in itself. After all, God himself bids Moses to make a graven image of a serpent (out of bronze) and instruct the snake-bitten Israelites to look on it to receive God's healing (Num 21:4-9). Two graven images of cherubim are also to grace the Ark of the Covenant, made at the express command of God Himself (Ex 25:19-20). Thus, the ban is not on the making of images as such, but on idolatry: "you shall not bow down before them or worship them". (Ex 20:5).

One can also nurture an "idolic" attitude towards words and books. If one believed, for instance, that a dogmatic formula had "once and for all" been able to capture within its linguistic boundaries God's very nature or some divine attribute, or even the elusiveness of faith experience, so as to be wholly irreformable, one is well on the road to making an idol of a dogma. As Gabriel Marcel so rightly put it, "misguided fidelity leads to idolatry". Ironically enough, those most guilty of this kind of idolatry are invariably well-intentioned and committed religious believers. Authentic dogmas, far from being the end-term and exhaustive expression of an experience, are rather the starting-point and guideline of a journey.

But such "linguistic idolatry" can be-and has been-committed by atheists and agnostics, too. Witness, for instance, Bertrand Russell's infamous "picture theory of language", as presented by him in *An Outline of Philosophy* (1927):[48]

> A spoken sentence consists of a temporal series of events; a written sentence of a natural series of bits of matter. Thus it is not surprising that language can represent the course of events in the physical world; it can, in fact, make a map of the physical world, preserving its structure in a more manageable form, and it can do this because it consists of physical events. But if there were such a world as the mystic postulates, it would have a structure different from that of language, and would therefore be incapable of being verbally described.

Nowadays, nobody would espouse such claims that language is an exact copy of reality, not even an adept of the positive sciences. And Russell was soon to repudiate this simplistic view. Try as he might to have bullied the early Wittgenstein to uphold his idolatrous theory of language, Russell wasn't quite able to make his protégé disavow the persistence of *das Mystiche* in experience and when the latter finally broke with such views in his *Philosophical Investigations,* Russell did not conceal his displeasure. "The symbol provides food for thought", remarked Ricoeur. Maybe it is because of our intellectual laziness that we all too often reduce the elusive symbol to the more

48 Bertrand Russell. 1927. *An Outline of Philosophy,* London: Allen and Unwin, p. 46.

manipulable idol. As Jean Lacroix has put it so well, "Idols must die, so that symbols can live".

All this cautions us as regards our attitude to any alleged "revealed book". Any such Holy Scripture cannot but be "Word of God, in words of man". And words are but human creations, sharing in all the limitations and inadequacies of the culture and historical moment with which they are bound up. In the normal course of events, one must needs make use of the latest tools of literary criticism-form criticism, historical criticism, redaction criticism, to name a few-so as to avoid naive and hasty interpretations. For those religions who describe themselves as "religions of the Book" in the strict sense (that is, in effect, they maintain that God has in some way become "incarnate" in a book) and thus see all such attempts to critically and scientifically study the Word so as to discover its meaning, they would have to approach the problem in a way analogous to Christian attempts to grasp-and explain to others-how a limited human form could embody the divine through the Incarnation. This might be a very fruitful and inspiring starting-point in dialogue.

Some Quotes

"By education most have been misled;
So they believe, because they were bred.
The priest continues where the nurse began,
And thus the child imposes on the man."

– John Dryden

"Nature is a temple in which living columns sometimes emit confused words. Man approaches it through forests of symbols, which observe him with familiar glances."

– Charles Beaudelaire

"Indeed the Idols I have loved so long have done my credit in this World much wrong:
Have drowned my Honour in a Shallow Cup and sold my Reputation for a Song."

– Edward Fitzgerald, *Rubáiyát of Omar Khayyám*

"I have not loved the world, nor the world me;
I have not flattered its rank breath, nor bowed
To its idolatries a patient knee,
Nor coined my cheek to smiles, nor cried aloud
In worship of an echo."

– George Gordon, Lord Byron

"(T)he mind of man is, if I may be allowed the expression, a perpetual factory of idols. ... The true state of the caseis that the mind of man, being full of pride and temerity, dares to conceive of God according to its own standard, and, being sunk in stupidity and immersed in profound ignorance, imagines a vain and ridiculous phantom instead of God."

– Jean Calvin

Chapter 8

TOWARDS A LIBERATIVE ETHIC

Introduction

The impact of religion and of religious leadership is felt by common people in another area of their life, besides that of worship and ritual. This is the whole sphere of how they should act in their day-to-day life, the controversial matter of morality. And, here too, the legacy of religion has not always been sweetness and light. If religion has frequently produced a Francis of Assisi or a Gandhiji, and been able to inspire women, children and men to heroic commitment in the service of the poor, the marginalised and the sick, it has also created Torquemada and added to the stock of human misery, paralysing generations and nations by sowing crippling feelings of guilt and fear in many a soul. Religious leaders have not infrequently been all too quick to issue fatwahs and hurl anathemas than seek to listen and understand. They have not often been of the type that would not crush the bruised reed or stamp on the smouldering ember. If there was a fictitious character who once remarked that, "If God did not exist, everything would be permitted", there are hosts of real life people whose only motive for not raping, murdering and looting the weak is the fear of God's punishment or the hope of His reward.

This, to say the least, is evidence of a very childish and retarded moral sense at work.

In this section, we take a look at three models of morality – three paradigms of how people live out their moral behaviour. All these are based on concrete experience. The first, according to me, is rankly oppressive. The other two are liberative, the first admitting of a theistic as well as an atheistic understanding. The second is very specifically religious: indeed, I will be explicating it from a particularly Christian perspective. I must add that I am heavily indebted to Louis Monden SJ and his insightful little book *Sin, Liberty and Law* for many ideas developed over here.[49]

The Oppressive Model: The Instinctive Level

The basis of this model is something totally external to the agent: the whole gamut of societal taboos and prohibitions laid down by the people among whom one has to live. This is how one derives his sense of moral law. Initially, one reacts against these prescriptions with understandable resentment and rebellion, seeing them as arbitrary encroachments on one's freedom of action imposed on him from the outside. But soon one's realises that resistance is useless: it'd be a hopeless case of "me against the world". The best course of action would be to capitulate, to submit before the irresistible force. Thence arises a sense of obligation, which is only an apparently inner motivation: it's nothing more than succumbing to society's brain-washing. This kind of "moral agent" is unable to explain why such-and-such an action is enjoined or forbidden – other than the fact that "they" require it. The "they" in question could be one's particular religion or concept of god, his circle of friends, employers, family or society at large, rightly or wrongly comprehended. One might note, in passing that this kind of morality is witnessed to by a well-trained, house-broken domestic pet. It has learned, from painful experience that it must not mess on the carpet. It does not quite grasp why it should not; it knows full well what'll happen if it does ... and that's enough for it!

49 Louis Monden. 1966. *Sin, Liberty and Law.* London: Dublin, G. Chapman.

In the same context, we can explain such a person's conscience as nothing but the stern warning of unpleasant memories: remember what happened when you did it last time? Better not do it again. Consequently, one's notion of sin and guilt would be linked up with having materially transgressed the law. There's no room for considering extenuating circumstances, intention, qualifying circumstances, etc. It's the literal fact of having done what was forbidden. How often, for instance, do we not hear, in confession, a penitent accusing himself of having "missed the Sunday obligation" because he had to take care of his ailing mother? To keep up our analogy with the house dog, straight after having messed on the carpet, its tail droops 'contritely' and, 'guilt-ridden', it crawls under the bed to await its inevitable punishment. From this we can see that contrition is none other than the fervent wish to avoid the terrible consequences of one's material transgression. Of course, it would be wonderful if the fact of one's having materially broken the law could be covered up. Indeed, one would be prepared to go to almost any lengths to ensure that-even risk breaking an even bigger taboo, if one could conveniently get away with it. But if there's no escape-the hapless cherry tree lies on its side and the offending axe wilts in my guilty hand before the irate gaze of my father-there's nothing else left for me to do but make a good confession: hopefully this abject self-accusation might melt the stem and just judge's heart. If not, then one must resign himself to face his punishment. a kind of harsh vengeance visited on him from an outside source, law wreaking its vengeance for having been spurned. Indeed, such punishment comes almost as a relief: once over, it means that the balance has been righted, one is back to a clean slate (hopefully the judge won't bear grudges) and does his best to assure the powers that be that he will be a model of approved good behaviour. This is none other than one's purpose of amendment. Never again will I transgress the prescriptions of the law and have to go through the whole harrowing experience again!

The Liberative Models: The Human Level

The first of these two liberative models is assuredly humanistic, but not necessarily religious, though such an interpretation is possible.

Thus it can be read as an expression of Kantian morality just as much as the explication of traditional Thomistic "natural law" ethics or even as the unfolding of the socially-oriented moral vision of an atheistic thinker like Camus.

The source of this moral sense is entirely internal: it all stems from the dynamic drive of one's deepest being. Thus, law is identified with self-development, self-realisation or total human growth and not some external code. In other words, I recognise that I owe it to myself to act in a way that is in accordance with my personal worth: thence comes the sense of obligation. Conscience would then be the critical and responsible use of mature discernment to decide whether a particular action would, in a concrete situation, enhance or impair my personal growth. I would recognise that, in certain cases, the context might justify my contravening the general guidelines of a law, as regards its material or literal requirements. Accordingly, sin would arise when I, consciously and deliberately, inflicted a wound on my being, hindering or frustrating my personal development due to cowardice or the craving for cheap popularity. Guilt would be the awareness of such a self-inflicted wound and the only punishment relevant to a person at this level would be the recognition that I have done harm to myself-for which I would feel sincere contrition and regret. Confession would be the humble admission that I have no one else but myself to blame for this. A strong purpose of amendment would follow, wherein I would resolve to do all within my power to make up for the loss of self-development. By that same token, I would make a firm resolve not to repeat such an action that would retard or hinder my human development.

The Religious Level

Here I am using the word "religious" in an exclusively theistic sense, that is, one presupposing an inter-personal relationship with God. As I have said above, I would like to spell it out in terms of the Christian vision, though it could equally be understood-with a few necessary changes-in terms of a non-Christian theistic religion, say Islam or Judaism. My only excuse for doing it this way is that I am a convinced Christian and these notes are being prepared primarily for young men and women who are convinced Christians, preparing themselves for a liberative mission in today's world.

If the basis of the oppressive-instinctive level of morality was wholly external, that of the liberative-humanistic type fundamentally internal, the liberative-religious model finds its roots in a dialogical relationship between the two. Here, the moral agent finds himself or herself personally addressed in the deepest depths of his or her being by the voice of understanding yet challenging Love amid the concrete circumstances of active life.

In place of law – whether it be the external demands of society or the inner drive of my own being – there is but a loving invitation. Thence derives my sense of obligation, the urge to respond adequately to such an inspiring vocation: the resolve to make and live out a total commitment is my natural, effortless response. I slowly begin to understand that I am being called to do more than "the merely human" (which, in itself, is quite a lot): it is a challenge to "go the extra mile", to return love for hate, to give more than what is "only reasonable". In Christian terms, it's a question of transcending the Ten Commandments for the Beatitudes. Conscience now becomes love, discerning with the lights of God's Spirit, what would be the most heroically loving, the most Christ-like way of answering the exigencies of the present existential situation. Sin would now be having said NO to such an opportunity and guilt the recognition that I did not have the courage and generosity to live up to the commitment of greater moment I had once made earlier. Contrition would be the agonising acknowledgement of this unworthy response, recognising that the loving, trusting invitation still endures. Thence follows confession of one's cowardice and inconstancy and a firm resolve to recommit oneself with greater fealty to the call of the One who remains ever faithful.

From Actions to Attitudes

Even the most cursory reading of the above would make it clear that the more a moral system stresses actions (based on laws) the nearer it approaches the oppressive end of the spectrum and the more it places an emphasis on attitudes (based on love), the closer it comes to the liberative end. Please note, I speak of emphasis, not exclusiveness:

actions and laws do have their legitimate place in any moral set-up, but the stress should rather be on the attitude out of which one's deeds flow.

Is all this dangerous, unorthodox thinking? I think not. No more so than was the practice of Jesus or any of the great prophetic figures or social reformers of history. They frequently castigated civic and religious leaders who encouraged and upheld an ethico-religious system based on shallow, external conformism and lip service, whereas the heart and intention was elsewhere. In fact, this was the thrust of Jesus' denunciations of pharisaic morality. After all, it's quite possible to go in for a lot of externally laudable activity for non-praiseworthy motives. Take a look at I Corinthians 13, where St Paul reminds us that it is possible to exhibit all signs of being endowed with impressive charismatic gifts, of distinguishing oneself as a generous almsgiver or an intrepid martyr for the faith-all out of questionable motives ("... and have no love"). This would render such feats morally worthless. It's a question of doing the truth in love. Besides, there could arise situations where love might require one to go against the exact prescriptions of the law (can a law foresee all possible qualifying and extenuating circumstances?), as when the traditional moralists concede, one is not obliged to return a weapon to its owner if he asks for it back under the influence of alcohol or a blind rage, or when a starving person takes by force from the abundant table of his opulent and anti-social neighbour. On the other hand, the demands of love might urge one to go beyond the call of the law and reason, as in the case of the heroic sacrifice of Maximilian Kolbe.

Of course, a lot depends on how one understands love, one of the most overworked words (along with freedom) in the average person's lexicon today. In the context of the philosophy of liberation, it refers to the active desire to promote the "being more" of all people and the resolve to denounce and undo all that, on the other hand, aims at the "having more" (or even the alleged "being more") of a few at the expense of the "being more" of others.

Faith and Justice

It is a sad legacy of the traditional soul-body dichotomy that has led to the fact that some men of religion thereby justify their alleged "neutrality" or non-involvement in human struggles against the corrupt status quo. Religion, they maintain concerns the soul and the hereafter (which alone comprise their "department"). Issues concerning the body and "worldly" realities are the responsibility of the layman exclusively and come under the purview of economics, politics and other "secular" disciplines, having nothing to do with religion and their honourable selves. In less polite circles, this sort of argumentation is called "covering one's backside" for there seems to be no scarcity of men of the cloth dabbling in political issues, so long as it is in favour of the established order. It is rather when clerics and religious side with the oppressed in denouncing the unjust status quo that fulminations against "priests and nuns dabbling in politics" are hurled about.

Humans, of course, are not susceptible to such dichotomies in the existential order. Indeed, as a recent Synod of Bishops, in their Statement on Justice in the World (1971) – anticipating the famous "Decree of the Thirty-Second General Congregation of the Society of Jesus" by some four years – put it, "Action on behalf of justice and participation in the transformation of the world fully appear to us as a constitutive dimension of the preaching of the Gospel". This was only put in a more succinct way by the famous statement, "the service of faith of which the promotion of justice is an absolute requirement", this being not just the "mission of the Society of Jesus today",[50] but that of the whole Church.

Religion and morality must concern the development and liberation of the entire human person, not just one allegedly "spiritual" part. All authentic religion seems to recognise this, calling for "the building up of God's Kingdom", "the establishment of Ram Rajya", or whatever, which-shorn of their communalistic misinterpretations"- echo the Marxist call for the creation of a classless, casteless society. It is the above-mentioned deplorable dichotomy that has led to the

50 *Documents of General Congregation XXXII of the Society of Jesus*, Decree. 4, No. 48.

scandalous spectacle of Latin American dictators being photographed devoutly praying at Mass in the front pews of the local Cathedral and then going off to dispatch death squads to eliminate troublesome clerics and religious leaders as well as reading in Indian newspapers how a corrupt, public official who had squandered state funds for private self-indulgence, made the police officials who had come to arrest her wait while she finished her elaborate and lengthy puja!

Nikolai Berdyaev's scathing remark would well be taken to heart by all religions: "Marxism bears witness to a forgotten task of Christianity." Because traditional Christians, like the pious practitioners of other religions, had over-spiritualised their mission, reducing their faith to the opium that assured them a piece of pie in the sky when they die, that Marx emerged as God's prophet, to be a voice for the *anawim*, turning the structures of the world upside down. However inadequate was his solution, it was a step in the right direction. And the collapse of the Communist Empire no more signals the failure of Marxism any more than the consumerist societies of the First World are a "proof" of their being the answer to the economic woes that they are creating for mankind.

The USSR was never an authentic realisation of Marx's vision, just as the "Christian nations" of the world never were really faithful to the vision of Jesus. And establishing a "free" market doesn't create a "free" nation!

Some Quotes

"Justice is such a fine thing that we cannot pay too dearly for it."

– Alain Rene Lesage

"Faith, of itself, if it does not have works, is dead."

– James 2:20

"Elegance is achieved when all that is superfluous has been discarded and the human being discovers simplicity and concentration: the simpler and more sober the posture, the more beautiful it will be."

– Paulo Coelho

"It's a hard world for little things."

– Davis Grubb

Chapter 9

TOWARDS A LIBERATIVE EROTICS

Introduction

For most people "erotics" would be seen as another word for "sexuality". Emmanuel Levinas prefers to see it as "broader and more comprehensive: erotic extends to non-sexual ambits, e.g. gluttony."[51] Here I am using the term as a means to study how humans relate to each other on the basis of gender.

A: Gender Discrimination Against Women

In General

While women, in general, constitute 50% of the world's population and make up one-third of the regular work force (this statistic, let it be emphasised, does not take into consideration the unpaid work of mothers, etc.), they end up actively toiling during two-thirds of all working hours, receiving in turn only one-tenth of total world income and owning less than one percent of world property. Indeed, in some parts of the world, as in Subsaharan Africa, women are

51 Quoted by Enrique Dussel. 1985. *Philosophy of Liberation*, trsl. Martinez and Markowsky, New York: Orbis Books, p. 67, footnote.

prohibited outright from owning, or exercising any proprietary rights over, property.

Particularly in the Third World...

Women are universal water-carriers, spending between one and four hours a day in fetching and transporting it in heavy pots or buckets balanced precariously on their heads. As we know from experience in our country, little girls, even before they are ten, are pressed into this toilsome service. In many rural areas-in India and elsewhere in the Third World-this is considered a "woman's job" and able-bodied husbands and sons have no scruple to make their frail womenfolk do this laborious work, even if the latter are ill or pregnant. The distance from one's home to a source of abundant and clean water is crucial to health and hygiene and less than 10% of rural Third World dwellers have easy access to this essential commodity. That number increases to 25% in urban areas of those nations and is frequently lower in some of our Indian cities.

Though women account for some 40% of the world's food production, some 75% of the malnourished people of the Third World are female. In such countries, women and girls are regularly passed over to ensure better sustenance to males. An indication of this is the comparative weights of women in first and Third World nations. If properly fed, all women the world over should exhibit the same growth levels. Yet an American woman, on an average, weighs 58 Kgs, while her Latin American and Indian counterparts tag along behind with 50 and 45 Kgs respectively.

Thus about 50% of all females in the Third World, from the ages of 15 to 49 are severely anaemic. The consequent physical depletion-aggravated by overwork and under-nourishment-results in greater risk of low birth-weight, which increases infant mortality by 30%. Mothers in developing countries, while doing the best they can for their off spring, with their limited resources of time, energy, income and knowledge, are in urgent need of drastic improvements in all these areas to ensure better health for their children ....and themselves! Nearly two out of three illiterate people in the world are women. Resistance of Third World women to opportunities of raising their quality of life, through better nutrition, family planning, domestic hygiene, are very closely associated with their illiteracy. As late as 1980, some 29 countries reported that over 80% of their women citizens were illiterate. And even though the number of girls in primary schools has risen significantly in most less developed countries it must be noted that girls attend school from one-half to one-tenth as frequently as boys of similar ages. Invariably, this is because girls are obliged to help with housework.

...But in the First World, Too!

When Taslima Nasrin sought refuge from the fundamentalists of Bangladesh in the liberal society of Scandinavia, she was appalled at the incidence of wife-beating there. Again, in First World countries, where women have managed to secure a footing in less traditional fields, they still find themselves as a disadvantage in the professions, even though they may be as qualified as their male counterparts. In the US, more than half of all women work outside the home, constituting almost half (42%) to be precise of the nation's work force. Yet, even there, they earn just over half of what male wage-earners do. Female accountants and lawyers, the best off, bring home only about 70% of their male colleagues' wages. Sexual harassment on the street and in the work place (even if it's the Oval Office!) is considerably less than in the Third World, but it persists there, too. Besides, there is a legacy of moral and psychological discrimination against women which refuses to die. Women today are more conscientised about it, but millennia-old prejudices won't go away too easily.

An Illustrious Lineage

The names of those who have fulminated against women since the dawn of recorded history reads-like a veritable *Who's Who* in the annals of international culture, drawing from such widely diverse fields as philosophy, theology, politics, psychology and literature. No mean number of saints and quite a few doctors of the church and popes would be found in their midst. This is not the place to cite the whole list or mention a few of the awful things they have dogmatically pontificated about feminine wiles and wickednesses. I shall but skim through such pronouncements of some of the more significant trend-setters of Western thought, who are generally assumed to be more liberal than our *deshi* variety.

During the Golden Age of classical Greek thought, when the nobler civilisation of Socrates-Plato-Aristotle laid the foundations of democracy and much else that was significant in the making of the European mind, women were looked down upon so much that homosexuality was considered to be the only sexual expression worthy of that noble creature, the male. It was considered quite unbecoming for someone so sublime as a male to feel love or passion for someone so inferior as a female! Only another man (or a young boy!) was considered to be fit for his amorous advances. Women one had to marry, for – alas! – the sublimest of homosexual liaisons could not assure one of an heir to the ancestral wealth and, besides, someone had to take care of the kids, run the household and cook the meals, while the masculine element was out at war or on the hunt, holding forth in the forum or courting some attractive teenage lad. Plato's famous dialogue on friendship, Lysis, is an unabashed endorsement of homosexual love, as illustrated by the unrestrained passion of Hippothales for the comely youth, Lysis.

Aristotle gave a pseudo-metaphysical basis to male chauvinism by alleging that a woman was a misbegotten male. In his celebrated treatise *On the Generation of Animal*,[52] he informs us sagely:

> The female's contribution [to reproduction] also is a secretion [as is the male's], and has all the parts in it potentially, though none of it actually; it has in it potentially even those parts which differentiate the female from the male, for just as the young of mutilated parents are sometimes born mutilated and sometimes not, so also the young born of a female are sometimes female and sometimes male instead.

A little later, the Stagyrite will go on to detail the various natural conditions that are supposed to "cause" a child to be female, rather than male. Among the "observed facts", allegedly noted by him, are the followings:

52 Vol. V of the Jowett-endowed translation of *Aristotle's Works into English*, Oxford: Oxford University Press, 1949 reprint. (IV, 2, 737a 27).

> ... More females are produced by the young and those verging on old age, than by those in the prime of life; in the former, the vital heat is not yet perfect, in the latter it is failing. And those of a moister and more feminine state of body are more wont to beget females, and a liquid semen causes this more than a thicker; now all these characteristics come of a deficiency in natural heat. Again, Mere males are bon if copulation takes place when north, rather than south, winds are blowing. For in the latter case, the animals produce more secretion, and too much secretion is harder to concoct; hence the semen of the males is more liquid, and so is the discharge of the catamania.[53]

Smith and Ross, the translators, in a footnote, feel constrained to add an embarrassed comment: "the facts given in this chapter are unluckily a mere string of popular fables". Aristotle was, of course, quits in the dark as regards genes and chromosomes, but that didn't hinder him from delivering his *magister dixit* with typical aplomb ... misleading European thought for over a millennium! Thomas Aquinas, in his *Summa*[54] cites "the Philosopher" in this connection but adds a mitigating clarification. It is actually "only as regards nature in the individual that the female is something defective and *manqué*)."[55] However, the Angelic Doctor goes on, more precisely, "with reference to nature in the species as a whole, the female is not something *manqué* (deficient), but it is .so according to the tendency of nature, which is directed to the work of procreation". Consciously or no, the ground was being led for a latter-day Nietzsche to come

---

53 Vol. V of the Jowett-endowed translation of *Aristotle's Works into English*, Oxford: Oxford University Press, 1949 reprint. (766b 30).

54 Thomas Aquinas. 2012. *Summa Theologiae Prima Pars, 1-49, The Complete Works of Saint Aquinas*. Lander, WY: Aquinas Institute for the Study of Sacred Doctrine and Aquinas, Thomas. 2012. *Summa Theologiae Prima Pars, 50-119, 14*. Lander, WY: Aquinas Institute for the Study of Sacred Doctrine. (Ia, 92, 1).

55 Translation of the Dominicans of the English-speaking Provinces of the Order, Volume 13, London, Blackfriars, 1963, p. 37: the Latin text reads *aliquid deficiens et occasionatum*.

on the scene and hold that a woman's sole claim to dignity is that she might, one day, be able to give birth to a man-child!

Later, in his *Politics*[56] Aristotle would inform us that a woman remains in a state of perpetual childishness, which fact requires her eternal subordination to the mature-adult male. He details two forms of natural subordination that abide forever: that of the (natural) slave to the (natural) master and that of woman to man. This natural subordination is justified, he tells us, inasmuch as both slaves and women are unable to reason well and so should be ever kept under the control of adult males who, being equipped with reason, can best direct them for their own good as well as that of the community at large.[57] Women are slightly better than natural slaves who are so radically deficient that even the former can command them. Thus, "although there may be exceptions to the order of nature [I suppose he's thinking of a female commanding a male slave], the male is fitter for command than the female, just as the elder and full-grown is superior to the younger and more immature". However, we are cautioned, this "exception to the order of nature" should never justify us thinking that women can ever become fit to command in general: their reason is never fully "effective" for they don't ever succeed in learning how to not allow it to be overcome by their passions and emotions. Thus, they should welcome being under the tutelage of men, who alone know how to function efficiently by reason.

A long list of churchmen and social reformers seem to have drawn inspiration from these "insights" of Aristotle, the great guru of the west. St Ignatius of Loyola, a man in many respects far ahead of his time, seems to have been guided by Aristotle more than the Holy Spirit when, in his *Spiritual Exercises*,[58] he compared the strategy of "the enemy" (i.e. -the devil) to that of a woman, who is "weak when faced by firmness, but strong in the face of acquiescence."[59] On the

---

56 Volume X of the *Collected Works*, above-mentioned.

57 I, ii, 1259 12.

58 Ignatius of Loyola, and George E. Ganss. 1991. *Ignatius of Loyola: The Spiritual Exercises and Selected Works, The Classics of Western Spirituality*. New York: Paulist Press, no. 325.

59 *Ibid.*

Protestant side, there is the radical firebrand reformer, John Knox, Ignatius own contemporary, the title of one of whose revolutionary tracts is significant enough: "*First Blast of the Trumpet against the Monstrous Regiment of Women*" (1558). There he argued that nature, as ordained by God, had forever disabled women from ruling authority by depriving them of those virtues which are essential to good rule: "Nature, I say, doth paint them further to be weak, frail, impatient, feeble and foolish; and experience hath declared them to be inconstant, variable, cruel and lacking the spirit of counsel and regiment". Assuredly he was only thinking of women like Mary "Queen of Scots", whose suzerainty over his motherland he refused to reckon, and not women like his mother! Let us resist the temptation to make a long list of relevant quotes from such heralds of liberal and radical thought as Rousseau, Marx and Freud that reveal them as arrant Male Chauvinistic Pigs (at least in their unguarded moments) as those whom we wouldn't be surprised to see in such company!

The examples of illustrious women of our time, Golda Meir, Indira Gandhi, Margaret Thatcher-whatever we may think of their policies-should be evidence that "females" can be as efficient commanders and controllers of males as their counterparts of the opposite gender and have exhibited a rare acumen and insightfulness, coupled with a certain rugged determination and a ruthlessness that we have been accustomed to associate with only the most virile and macho of military generals. Not that such example were lacking in the past: witness Joan of Arc, Queen Boadicea, Lucrezia Borgia and our own Jhansi ki Rani. Unfortunately, most of us prefer to ignore such "observed facts" and prefer to follow the "popular fables" of the ancients and the medieval, as if they were scientific conclusions drawn from the latest empirical studies.

Many of the common religious taboos against women, particularly those prohibiting them to enter sacred spaces, stem from antiquated superstitions linked with their monthly emission of blood. Since blood was looked upon with awe and reverence in ancient times – a timely caution, no doubt to deter those blood-thirsty vendettas-the fact that women, uncontrollably, should shed so mysterious and sacred a commodity, led to their being viewed as temporarily or permanently ritually impure and thus unworthy of entering such places of worship. Nowadays, we know that the basis of such bans is ridiculous and un-founded, yet we prefer to scraps the bottom of the barrel for pseudo-theological and pseudo-psychological rationalisations to justify the maintenance of the status quo in this regard.

Double Standards

For long have women and girls been obliged to submit themselves to an unfair moral code that took a more lenient attitude to certain human failings if they were indulged in by men, but regarded these same peccadilloes as major crimes, when women were the "guilty" party! Though such an approach is on the way out in more enlightened societies, at home and abroad, it has the unfortunate habit of rearing its ugly head in the most unlikely places from time to time.

For instance, smoking and drinking are unsavoury and unhealthy habits in more senses than one. However, if a teen-age boy-or even an adult married man-is known to indulge in these to excess, the normal reaction would be a shrug and a remark to the effect that, "Well, boys will be boys!" And, if the misbehaving male were an adult, a husband and father, and would so lose control of himself as to puke on the floor and roll into the nearest convenient gutter, this would often elicit further comments to the tune of his, no doubt, having to face a shrewish wife at home and an unbearable work place. And if there is an erring male who is known to be a bit of a flirt, why this would just about make him a legend in his own life-time! Semi-admiring, implicit-affectionate terms like "naughty boy" and "young rogue" will be showered on him from all sides and he ends up feeling quite lionised by the whole thing.

But, let it be known that a particular woman or girl smokes, had even just once got a bit too tipsy at a party or indulged herself in a little mild flirtation and her fate is sealed, her reputation is tarnished forever and she is side-lined by the many, as if she were some modern-day Jezebel trying to come in out of the cold! Nobody will make excuses or indulgent remarks in her favour! Even though many a woman has to face severer tensions than the average man, no one will talk about extenuating circumstances in her case. Indeed, given the fact that women seem to cope, quite valiantly, with so much stress and pressure, without having to take recourse to alcohol, drugs or nicotine as easily and frequently as men ... we might well wonder which sex more merits the title of the "weaker" one!

Women in the Bible

The first book of the Bible, Genesis-revered by the faithful of three of the world's great religions presents a rather liberative vision of woman, popular opinions aside. This becomes all the more pronounced when we compare the Adam and Eve story with the classical myths of origin found in other traditions. Not infrequently, woman, in the latter cases, is shown as being made out of, or emerging from, some inferior part of the first man (invariably the first to be created, in all such tales). Ancient Far Eastern myths represent the first woman as being fashioned by the demiurge from out of man's foot, or from the clippings of his recently pared fingernails, or even out of the effluvia deposited from a mighty sneeze! In *Genesis*, however, Eve is made out of the sleeping Adam's rib (Gen 2:21). Jewish scholars tell us-and let us not forget that the Bible was originally a Jewish book, written for a Jewish audience, in a Semitic language, using Semitic idiom, that the rib-symbol bears a two-fold message. First, it means that, since the rib is closest to the heart, woman must be kept close to man's heart, that is, she must be loved and cherished – a timely piece of information for the sexual heirs of Plato, and Aristotle! Second, inasmuch as the rib cage also protects the heart from rough handling, subsequent injury and possible death, we are to conclude that there would be a context where woman protects man, that is, where she is the stronger sex! This would make the male chauvinists among us sit up and take notice! And, if my interpretation is correct (following that of Jewish scholars), *this* is what God's revelation is telling us: *this* is what we who "believe in the Bible" are expected to believe! Of course, many would prefer to hedge the issue by getting bogged down in a side question as, for example, whether we are justified in doing a non-literal reading of the "Creation myth" or whether monogenism or polygenism is more feasible, etc. Better to object to this rendering, than have to accept its disconcerting implications! This version, incidentally, would seem to be confirmed by the fact that Adam was promised by Jahveh-God that he (God) would make him (Adam) "a helpmate" (2:18). This is a clumsy translation of a Hebrew turn of phrase that could, more accurately, if also more circumlocutously, be rendered, "I will give him one who will need to lean on him when she is weak and on whom he will need to lean when he is weak".

For most of us, it is, of course, father exasperating that *Genesis* doesn't go on to detail exactly wherein lie these alleged feminine strengths: apparently, that's for us to figure out by ourselves. Basing myself on my own experience of the strengthening I have received from some very wonderful women in my life, I find that St John's Gospel suggests at least two possible areas where we men can turn to women for support in times of crisis. These concern those two occasions where Jesus is depicted as addressing Mary as *woman*. I am quite aware, of course, of John's theology and of the messianic implications of his use of the title: Cana and Calvary are two key moments of Jesus' exercise of his Christic vocation. In the former he gave the "first sign" of his salvific identity and in the latter he is seen as accomplishing it in a climactic moment. In both, he salutes Mary, the "woman", thanks to whom he has been able to become the messianic "Son of Man". Granting all this, I do not think I am quite off the mark in suggesting that we might also see Jesus as gracing Mary with that name because, on each occasion, she was bearing witness to a typical womanly strength: attention to little detail (at Cana, she noticed the lack of wine) and a superior ability to handle situations of stress and tension (at Calvary, for three long hours she *stood* – John is quite explicit on the point-by her son's side). Don't we come across situations in life where we men, are so preoccupied with the overall picture, the rational universal law, that we miss little details that might demand attention and somewhat different treatment? And haven't we, more than once, been forced to admit how our predominantly male decision-making system suffers from not taking into consideration insights into little detail that feminine perceptivity would have brought to our attention? Again, it is pretty obvious that men are physically stronger than women (the occasional female wrestler or body-builder aside), but have we never noticed how, in times of prolonged mental stress and tension, it is women who can handle the situation more effectively? Fewer widows and jilted girls take recourse to drugs and drinks and suicide to handle their heart-break than men, in similar situations, do. And countless Indian women live with remarkable endurance all kinds of abuse and torture from oppressive in-laws and husbands, and with courage and a cheerful exterior, bring up the children and struggle to put them through school!

Whether my latter hermeneutics is right or not, it seems to be clear enough that *Genesis* is presenting us with a very liberative – and challenging vision of woman, one that is part and parcel of divine revelation, to boot! What one could contest is whether the two areas of feminine strength I have proposed are in any way universal or whether I am hastily generalising from my limited personal experience.

Conclusion

It should be clear by now that, there is absolutely no foundation for the popular assumption, entrenched in uncritically received religious and pseudo-psychological data, that women are, in any way, inferior to men and hence need to remain ever under their guidance and control for their own and everyone else's good. The "metaphysical" and "religious" justifications trotted out to give an aura of argument in their favour have been found to be totally baseless, grounded on gratuitous and questionable impressions that might have been excusable in earlier, less enlightened times, but today, to say the least, are quite ridiculous. Apart from that, the witness of a host of illustrious women of personality, character and acumen, which fill the pages of history in every age and culture, should be evidence enough to the fact that these "theories" are nothing more than that-airy fairy theories, spun out of the prejudices that some male psyches feel they must fashion whenever they are faced with something different, hence, difficult to comprehend. An insecure psyche will feel threatened by such, and attack them mercilessly-be it a different sex, a different skin-colour or a different culture.

B: Gender Discrimination Against Homosexuals

Introduction

We call them by a host of discriminatory names and each generation has its own set of derogatory expressions for them: homos, faggots, queers, gays (not to mention *chhaka*. our own local variety-which actually means a eunuch). For most of us, any of these terms summons up an image of a sloppy, effeminate "fairy" or an inveterate child-molester-perhaps a frustrated cleric. The fact that the vast majority of child-molesters are heterosexually inclined is conveniently forgotten (as is also the fact that a very small proportion of sexual aggressions are committed by clerics). Again, lots of people think that *homosexual* refers exclusively to males who have a sexual preference for their fellows, wrongly assuming that the word comes from the Latin word, *homo* (man), which has given us words like homicide. Actually, it comes from the Greek *homos* (same), which have given us words like homogeneous and others of that ilk.[60]

Homosexual "Types"

Let me begin by stressing the fact that not all male homosexuals are effeminate in their gestures and walk, nor are all lesbians (female homosexuals) of the "female wrestler" type. I have had occasion to meet and counsel a good number of men and boys who acknowledge a preferential sexual attraction to males and many of these were quite "manly" and athletic. Some were even body-builders and expert boxers. I have encountered relatively less lesbians, but the few I have equally bear out the same impression, *mutatis mutandis*, for the other group, too.

The medical fraternity doesn't see one single cause as the basis of homosexuality. Recent medical research has indicated that it

60 Editor's Note: Please note that this book was composed in 1990 and so some of the latest developments in the LGBT community and legislations could not be taken into account. It is remarkable to note that Sashi Tharoor MP, one of the students of the author at St. Xavier's College, Kolkata, attempted to introduce a bill in the Indian Parliament, decriminalizing gay sex, which was not admitted in December 2015. The bill was a private member's Bill that sought to to amend Section 377 of the Indian Penal Code (IPC).

could be-at least in some cases-a matter of hormone's. Some aver that this would account for the "girly" type of homosexual only, not the others. It is more than likely that homosexuality stems from a variety of possible causes. Many counsellors and psychologists see a psychological, rather than a genetic reason, for such a tendency-over-identification with the parent of the opposite sex, lack of inspiring gender role models and so on. Sometimes, such influences appear to be not too deep and permanent, as in the case of one whose homosexual orientation is the result of fears in dealing with, and relating to, the other sex. Not a few are of the opinion that we would soon be in a position to "cure" homosexuality with hormone injections. Of course, this presupposes that homosexuals be prepared to view themselves as "diseased" people in need of a "cure", which is not always the case!

This last point is important, for many homosexuals do not view their condition in terms of a malady ("clumsy-hormone-sickness"?) that has to be remedied, any more than would left-handed people regard their eccentricity in a world of predominantly right-handed people (just for the record, I deny the parity, here: the comparison is a common one used by homosexuals themselves). What we easily tend to forget is that homosexuals did not *choose* their sexual orientation, "just for the sheer perversity of it", as one very dogmatic straight once averred to me. According to them, they discover it in their early teens and require no little time to realise that not everyone gets equally "turned on" by handsome hunks as they do. Homosexuality is neither the result of a vicious and malicious choice, nor is it even the outcome of a helpless situation into which they have gradually landed themselves through a series of previous uncontrolled and excessive acts, like your average drunkard or drug addict.

We have already had occasion to draw attention to that kind of "sociological homosexuality" found in excessively macho and belligerent societies in the past (and not too uncommon in Nazi Germany), which resulted from the glorification of masculine beauty and strength as against the more refined and refining "feminine" virtues. And Freud also mentioned the three phases of sexual awareness that everyone has to pass through in the process of maturing: the autosexual, the homosexual and the heterosexual.

One wonders whether a good deal of homosexual harassment and persecution would not stem from an unconscious rejection of such unmentionable tendencies in the oppressor.

If not every homosexual male is a "sloppy girlie", nor every lesbian a body-building battle-axe, neither is every homosexual some kind of uncontrollable sex maniac, whose relentless libido would drive him/her to deflower any hapless minor of the same sex that innocently comes his/her way.' Licentious homosexuals there are indeed are and they flit from sexploit to sexploit like the proverbial butterfly from flower to flower ... just as there are also plenty of licentious heterosexuals of the same stamp. But, just as it would be grossly unfair to tar all "straights" with the same brush of promiscuity, because a few are like that, so also is it blatant injustice to assume that all homosexuals are ditto! By far the vast majority of heterosexuals are able to behave quite honourably with the opposite sex and are quite capable of controlling any baser urges that might naturally manifest themselves on occasion. So it is with the average homosexual. There is no reason (or evidence) to conclude that homosexuals are more "sexed" or are lacking in self-control!

All this is meant to sensitise us to the plight of the homosexual in today's world. Do we realise the tensions, the injustices and the sufferings that such people are prey to, for no fault of their own? They are even more discriminated against than women and are subjected to verbal and physical abuse with indignity. Misrepresented, misunderstood and caricatured in the popular mind and in trashy literature, they are taught to despise themselves and to see themselves as even the object of divine wrath and malediction. They live in mortal fear of being "found out" and struggle to hide their identity and their most personal agonies from their families and their closest friends, for fear of possible rejection by those they love and who, until then, had loved and accepted them. If they are "brave enough" or "authentic enough" to "come out of the closet", they are immediately subjected to scorn and denied many basic human rights, such as freedom from violence and the right to housing and employment. It would be a gross injustice to ignore the plight of such marginalised people in our treatment of *The Philosophy of Liberation*!

We are admittedly venturing on dangerous ground and this is an issue on which is it difficult to speak dispassionately. The discourse is fraught with the possibility of being hastily judged, misquoted and of being dubbed a covert homosexual oneself. But, for all that, one cannot turn back. I hear a very strong and pastoral call for help: it is one of the signs of our times and we cannot brush it aside.

Gay Rights: What Are They?

The movement to claim certain "gay rights" started in the US in the seventies and soon spread to other countries as well. Slowly "gays" began to throw off a sense of indignity and "come out of the closet" demanding that they be afforded the same respect and freedoms that "straights" enjoyed. Thus, even in India-including Mumbai and our own Pune-there are (still somewhat clandestine) associations to help homosexuals find their identity and express themselves. Several homosexuals in and around Pune' allowed themselves to be named, quoted and even photographed by a local magazine that was running a feature on their situation. Not all gay demands may be equally acceptable and, very often, the manner in which some aggressive activists do make their pleas known are admittedly uncouth, abrasive and offensive. But this is not an uncommon initial behaviour found among groups that have long submitted meekly to all manner of injustice and are, at least beginning to find their voice and express centuries of suffering and indignation (to say the least). Thus many people were understandably "put off" by the aggressive lesbianism and "burning of bras" by some early "women's libers". Again, we often head people grumbling against the rude and offensive attitude and behaviour of "SCs and BCs" who've been allotted position of authority in Government service. But this is perhaps the inevitable price that society must be prepared to pay for having spurned, ignored and trampled underfoot such groups for so many generations. Besides, can we blame these men and women, newly come to power, who take as their role models others in power whom they have met (and who have meted out to them similar – if not worse! – treatment)? The fact is, however, such strident activism ends up by being the worst enemy of the very movements whose cause it champions or whose rights it claims: it provides fodder to the arguments of the ultra-conservatives who are at pains to prove to us all that, these people are the spawn of the devil and nothing but social collapse will result from "tolerating" and "encouraging" all this moral turpitude" perpetrated by people who are clearly (at least in their opinion!) "condemned and rejected by God"!

Let us now consider the various demands made by homosexual groups and lobbies for what they see as their legitimate rights. In this, we must try to proceed with level-headedness, handling delicate issues, as far as possible, dispassionately, without exaggeration and without hyperemotionalism. It will not be easy.

Claim I: The Right of Gays to Protection from Unprovoked Violence.

This, I would imagine, would be the least controversial of all such claims. It is a right due to every resident of a nation, including foreign visitors. I am not speaking, here, of homosexuals who might be said to have provoked such violence by indulging in sexual activity in public or even trying to solicit unwary passers-by. The fact is that there are a fair number of people, including law enforcement officials, who seem to think that any known homosexual is, by that token alone, fair game, for verbal and even physical abuse. Gays who have dared to "come out the closet" and publicly aver their inclination are pounced upon, harassed, severely beaten up and often even killed (as happened recently in a US case that hit the international headlines). And this is invariably done by self-appointed vigilantes who have taken the "law" into their own hands and have resolved to "personally punish" such people for their "wicked identity". Religious fundamentalists are the chief offenders here, but they do not hold a premium on fulfilling the role of such self-appointed moral police. Even in First World Canada, a recent study revealed that in 56% of cases where gays sought legal protection from such attacks, found the behaviour and response of the officers corned "markedly unsatisfactory."[61] Have we reason to believe that police in India would be more sympathetic?

---

61 Leahy, Michael P. T. and Dan Cohn-Sherbok. 1996. *The Liberation Debate: Rights at Issue*. London; New York: Routledge, p. 95.

I submit that homosexuals have as much right as heterosexuals to be protected from arbitrary violence and the mere declaration of one's homosexuality cannot be counted as reasonable provocation for "punishment" by anyone. However the Indian Penal Code, while not recognising the profession of homosexual identity as a cognisable Offence, does see homosexual acts, even in private and between consulting adults, as illegal.

And now we enter into stormy waters, because the next claim of homosexuals is directed against what they see as the injustice of precisely that illegality. And this is the next demand that we must take into consideration.

Claim II: Give Right of Gays to Sex Between Consenting Adults without Criminal Penalties

In 1967, Britain repealed a law of long standing: the law which was directed against "unnatural sex" (defined as sexual activity between members of the same sex), even if the offenders had been "consenting adults". Many US States and not a few European nations have made similar adjustments in their legal codes. Thus in all of these countries, it is no longer punishable by law for consenting adults to indulge in homosexual activity. Is this a good thing or a bad thing?

Understandably, the first reaction of most people, on hearing this would be indignation and disgust at this further evidence of the decline and fall of public morals. But, as we had suggested earlier, let us try to approach this contentious issue calmly and critically. If heterosexual activity between consenting adults is *not* a cognisable offence in a particular legal system, why should the same activity between consenting homosexual adults be punishable by law? After all, there are hosts of people who are quite convinced that extra-marital sex is immoral, but these are not in the least disturbed by the fact that there is no legal sanction for those heterosexuals (whose name is legion) who do that very thing. Why should only homosexual activity between consenting adults be singled out as criminal and punishable by law? The mere fact that a certain act is not regarded as illegal does not in the least, imply that it is therefore necessarily moral! It is not within the State's purview to decide the morality or immorality of certain kinds of behaviour: that is the responsibility of religious leaders, ethicians and others of that stamp. After all, a good many acts which the State declares to be illegal are not at all immoral, but are enforced only to ensure the smooth running of society (e.g. travel out of, or into, the country without proper documents). And some of the actions which the state does not hold to be illegal are, in the eyes of many citizens, immoral, all the same (e.g. abortion in some States, not to mention homosexual activity between consenting adults in others). It seems a gross injustice for heterosexuals to let heterosexuals go legally scot free for doing something they consider to be immoral, while they wish to impose legal punishment on homosexual consenting adults who are but doing the same thing!

Claim III: The Right to be Free from Discrimination in Housing Employment and Education

As regards discrimination against homosexuals in matters of housing, the usual argument on the grounds that it would encourage wanton behaviour and soliciting, seems markedly unfair. Lewd behaviour in public of any kind homosexual, or heterosexual, is a criminal offence and there exist legal sanctions to deal such offenders. And just as people would grant to heterosexuals the right to have sexual activity in the privacy of their own homes (between consenting adults, of course!), why shouldn't they grant the same right to homosexuals? There is no reason or empirical data to substantiate the assumption that homosexuals in a high rise apartment would do all manner of indecencies in public, while taking it for granted that heterosexuals never would. And the unreasonable fear that "kids and hapless teens" might be in danger if there were "a faggot in the building", could on the same grounds, be advanced against having "straights" in the complex? After all, statistics show that by far the majority of child abusers and sexual harassers are heterosexual males! But no one would dream of banning housing to that entire category! And if a solitary homosexual is found guilty of any such indecency, he should be punished by already existing laws that forbid lascivious activity in public. But this would not justify refusing housing to all future homosexuals on that account (unless one were ready to proceed in a similar manner whenever a heterosexual is caught in such an act).

A better argument for refusing to rent flats to homosexuals would be when the landlord concerned could claim that such would go against his/her religious convictions. After all, some fundamentalist Christians (not to mention others) see homosexuality as evil and practising homosexuals "living in a state of serious sin". Hence to rent a flat to such persons, knowingly, would be, so the argument runs, approving such behaviour. To oblige one to do so, against his/her religious convictions would infringe one's right to religious freedom, which just about every Constitution allows. This does not seem to be a valid argument to me but, since it touches on complex issues of jurisprudence and religion, it would best be dealt with by lawyers and moral theologians (and scripture scholars) in dialogue. It is interesting to note that a recent US Supreme Court decision went against such an argument made by an Alaskan landlord who had refused to rent out his flat to an unmarried heterosexual couple!

As regards employment, it seems to me that there is even less justification to discriminate against properly qualified homosexuals, here. That they might solicit, or sexually harass, fellow workers is a hypothetical charge that might equally be made against potential heterosexual employees. And, let us underline the fact, once again, that the majority of rape and sexual harassment cases have been recorded as 'being perpetrated by heterosexual males. It would be more logical (but very poor policy) to discriminate against all "straight males" as regards employment. Sexual harassment is a criminal offence and should be dealt with forthwith as per the sanctions of existing law: these are sufficient to cover all such cases justly and fairly.

Perhaps one should at least ban homosexuals from the teaching profession. But, once again, there have been numerous cases of sexual abuse of the young by heterosexuals. The fact is that both heterosexual and homosexual teachers may discover, from time to time, that they feel sexually aroused by some of their students. In such a case, both must (and equally can!) control, or sublimate, such urges-as, indeed, the overall majority do!

But the real point made in the claim that there be no discrimination against homosexuals in education life should be aimed more at the curriculum and what is taught. Teachers of Religion, Literature and Psychology (to mention but a few areas where the issue may come up) are not being asked to "justify and encourage" homosexuality, but are called upon to despatch all popular prejudices and "old wives' tales" about the wickedness of the homosexual, how he/she is nothing more than a walking, sexual appetite. In no unclear terms should it be pointed out that any kind of verbal or physical abuse and torture of homosexuals on that count alone is immoral and utterly unjustifiable. While respecting the religious sensibilities of those who are convinced that homosexuality is evil, it could be stressed that the average homosexual doesn't wilfully choose his/her sexual orientation, any more than the; average cancer patient did not "choose" his/ her malady. If one is determined to see homosexual orientation as an evil (such as cancer), one is hardly justified in branding the "sufferer" as evil on that grounds alone! One might even agree that homosexuality is "unnatural" in the sense that human sexuality is ordained to the production of children through love and the complementarity of the sexes is a necessity both for the mature realisation of authentic human love as well as for the integral growth of a child, later on. One could go into the more difficult question as to how we would counsel and guide such persons. There should be clear evidence of a helping, understanding hand being offered to youngsters who, about the time they first receive sex education classes are becoming aware of their sexual orientation. The right type of non-judgmental, supportive counselling may save youngsters years of pain and heart-break.

Claim IV: The Right to Military Service – And, Let Me Add – also the Right to Be Admitted to the Priesthood and Religious Life

To avoid useless recrimination and accusation, let me make it clear from the onset, that I am not implying that each and every homosexual who wishes to enter the military or the Church must be readily admitted! Obviously not. What I am saying is that anyone who has given evidence that he/ she is a fit candidate for the military or the ministry, having passed all the usual tests should not be rejected on the mere grounds that he/she has a homosexual inclination.

As regards admission to the military, let us note that the armed forces of many nations have long since opened their ranks to homosexuals, notably Germany, France, Israel, Switzerland, Sweden, Denmark, Norway, Finland, the Netherlands, Belgium, Australia, Spain and Canada. I have already pointed out that the popular stereotype of a homosexual as an "effeminate fairy" is unfair. If and when there is evidence of any or sexual harassment within ranks, action could – and should – be taken against them as it has frequently been found necessary to do so as regards guilty heterosexuals, in armies open to admitting women, too; there are legal sanctions within and without the armed forces to handle such offenders. The mere possibility of such an offence occurring should hardly be reasonable grounds for a blanket ban on all homosexuals, for by that same token there would have to be a parallel ban on all homosexuals from the army (and the number of cases of heterosexual harassment is far higher than that of the homosexual variety). Indeed, were one to have excluded all heterosexuals from the army as a cautionary preventive, arising from the spate of such scandals in the US army, the American armed forces would have been rendered extinct some years ago'

As for homosexuals entering the priesthood or religious life, in the first place, one should not be unduly surprised to hear that homosexuals could actually seriously consider such an option. Many homosexuals are as religious as their heterosexual fellows and not a few of them view their condition as a "cross" they have to bear, as others bear blindness or deafness. Many take their faith seriously and have a deep prayer life, seeking opportunities for commitment and loving service of their neighbour. Among them, there are not a few who do feel a vocation from God to the priesthood and/ or religious life beckoning them on. What should be our response to such candidates?

In the new code of Canon Law, there is no explicit ban on homosexuals being admitted to priestly or religious formation. Canon 1024 merely lays down that "only a baptised man can validly receive sacred orders". And Canon 643 does not list homosexuality as one of the disqualifications for valid admission to the religious life, though it recognises the right of an institute's law to "constitute other impediments even for the validity of admission". It must be emphasised that when we are speaking here of homosexuals, we are referring only to those who have such an inclination: the norms of priestly celibacy and religious chastity would preclude from entry anyone-homosexual or heterosexual-who intends to practise any sexual activity therein.

The Catechism of the Catholic Church assures us, rather bluntly, "Homosexual persons are called to chastity"[62] presumably, it is God who has called them to that state, by the mere fact that they discover a homosexual orientation in themselves. But what of non-Christian and atheistic homosexuals, who would see no value in such chastity? Why would they be "called" to such a state, by virtue of a personality trait that is no choice of their own? Where would be the basis of that freedom which is supposed to be the foundation for embracing that lifestyle? But let us leave this point for critical discussion a little later. If we were, for the sake of argument (and only for the sake of argument) to grant that, at least, all Catholic homosexuals are called to chastity, can we legitimately and in justice refuse admission to the priesthood or the religious life to those who feel convinced that they have a divine vocation to these states of life? The *Catechism* goes on to say, "By the virtues of self-mastery that teach them inner freedom, by prayer said sacramental grace, they can and should gradually and resolutely approach Christian perfection."[63] These lines are applicable to all who would enter religious life or the priesthood and are tantamount to accepting that homosexuals have the wherewithal to live out a genuine vocal in the ecclesiastical ministry.

Of course, inasmuch as the homosexual would be living in close proximity with those to whom he could be sexually attracted, does make his situation more fraught with "temptation", difficulty and danger. But, nourished by a deep life of prayer and companionship with the Lord, a healthy understanding of asceticism and personal sacrifice and guided by superiors and spiritual guides who are understanding and supportive, it can be done. I have had occasion to meet and guide many priests and religious who had been allowed to enter at an early age and discovered their sexual orientation only after

62 Catholic Church. *Catechism of the Catholic Church.* Liguori, MO: Liguori Publications, 1994, no. 2359.

63 *Ibid.*

ordination or profession. I can state, quite categorically that by far the overwhelming majority have learnt to live quite joyfully and with a deep and inspiring commitment to the service of people of all ages and both sexes. Empirical data seem to bear out the fact that there is greater likelihood of heterosexual abuse than of the homosexual variety!

Claim V: The Right to Marriage and the Legal/Social Benefits of Marriage

Already in Denmark, Sweden, Norway, Finland and, very recently, the Netherlands and Canada, homosexuals have the legal right, to enter into marriage and claim all the usual tax, inheritance and other civil benefits accruing thereby. In other countries, homosexual couples make a kind of commitment to each other and have had these "marriage vows" solemnised in religious ceremonies recognised by neither the State nor any of the main line churches, yet they, too, are pressing for legal recognition, precisely because they wish to lay claim to these privileges and benefits, too. Many homosexual couples who say that they have lived together for many years, loyally and faithfully, are saddened and hurt to realise that they are denied the social benefits that any heterosexual couple can, even if the latter's marital life and commitment leaves much to be desired.

The Norwegian Ministry of Children and Family Affairs has provided us, perhaps, with the most forceful official argument in favour of homosexual marriage when, in support of that country's pertinent law of 1993, it wrote, "It can be detrimental for a person to have to suppress fundamental feelings, concerning attachment ,and love for a person. Distancing oneself from these feelings or attempts to suppress them may destroy one's self-respect". In parsing, let me point out that it is not clear to me why two people must *either* acknowledge their love and affection for each other through marriage or "distance themselves" from each other: love and affection can be acknowledged and celebrated in other ways than marriage and sexual union. Whatever, homosexual couples aver that, like traditional married couples, they too wish for stable marital unions, desire to live together in harmony and intimacy and seek to support each other every day, materially, financially and emotionally.

One can appreciate the unenviable situation of homosexuals. Those who cannot, for whatever reason, accept that "they are called to chastity" (as the Church feels convinced that they are) are in a quandary. What should they do? Some, too afraid to reveal their real identity, seek a quasi-fulfilment in a heterosexual marriage, trying to "make the best of it": indeed, some among them have children, but live in a state of basic sexual frustration, while trying their best to make their spouses happy, pretending to enjoy their love for each other in its sexual expressions. Very often, they seek compensation in homosexual dalliances on the sly ... only to be burdened with threats and blackmail! Others resign themselves to a basic loneliness, seeking to find meaning in Platonic friendships (no easy thing for one who cannot make sense of the ideal of chastity): "What is life, without lovers and only friends!" a gay friend of mine complained to me bitterly and, though he gave me his full attention, he could not resonate with what I had to say about celibacy. Still others launch themselves on a hectic binge of promiscuity and find life hollow and empty, as well might we expect. Still others boldly "take the plunge" and form a partnership with another male, finding meaning in their mutual love. But thereby, they have to face ostracism by their families, other friends and their own religion-no easy burdens to bear, (especially in India). And, to crown it all, as we have noted, however stable and loyally committed their difficult union may be, they are deprived of all the legal and social benefits that the shallowest and most hypocritical of heterosexual marriages can claim! No wonder the feel that the dice are loaded against them.

But, when all is said and done, can we give an absolute and equivocal endorsement to homosexual marriages? After all, marriage is a good deal more than a life-long commitment of' love (such as between even heterosexual friends). It involves the celebration of such love through the complementarities of gender, psychology and sexuality. It is the discovery of the mysterious "other" of the person of the opposite sex. It is the bringing up a couple's very own children, the very incarnation of their love for each other. It is the bestowing of these children the secure environment of the love of husband and wife for each other and of father and mother for the offspring. It is providing children with an upbringing with the male and female playing complementary roles in all this, as also offering their children viable role models. No family is able to give children a perfect experience of this ideal-but, then, it is not required that it be so!

However, it is one thing to recognise that many heterosexual do not succeed in living out the full meaning of what married life is about and quite another thing to have to admit that homosexual marriages simply *cannot* do it (assuming that marriage, in the fullest sense, does involve all what I have just listed)! Is there any evidence that homosexual couples, in spite of not being able to experience, and witness to, this "fuller unfolding of marriage life" can and do find happiness and fulfilment (as least in some appreciable measure)? If there were, maybe we could, at least on a "trial" basis, give legal recognition to certain homosexual unions, treated on an individual level, The fact that so many heterosexual marriages do end up "on the rocks" may be more of a sign that the type of consumerist and individualistic ethos that we are developing today is ill-suited to form people for mature commitment, rather than that something is wrong with the traditional family concept. On the other hand, the "homosexual marriage" experiment is rather recent (barely ten years old) and it may be far too soon to take the data conclusively: a pioneering venture requires some "leeway time" before it can settle down and prove its worth!

Claim VI: The Right to Adopt and/or to Retain Custody of Children

The Asian Age of November 16, 1998, informs us, that the Netherlands has just joined the small group of Scandinavian nations that grants this legal right to homosexual couples. This is the last, and probably the most strongly contested, of all homosexual rights, no doubt because it involves the welfare of a third party-an innocent child! In favour of this claim, proponents put forward the following data. First, there is already the fairly widespread fact that children are being raised by many homosexual couples, as their own. So it is no mere "hypothetical problem". A 1970 survey in California, USA, revealed that as many as 20% of all male homosexual couples and a third of all female homosexual couples had been married and retained their children even after terminating their heterosexual union and later contracting some form of stable homosexual commitment. And, we are assured that the children “showed no difference from other groups, either in sexual orientation or in general, mental health.”[64] Confirmation of this seems to come from a recent BBC programme on the condition of children raised by homosexual couples. Indeed, Posner goes on to note, “children raised by an unmarried heterosexual woman had more psychological problems.”[65] Of course, as even the advocates of this right have to admit, samples have been small and have covered a relatively short time-span. All the same, they, venture to ask, is it justified that children should be removed from the custody of a parent who loves and cares for them successfully, merely on the grounds that he/she has begun to live in a homosexual liaison? A common objection is to the effect that children raised by homosexual partners would inevitably become the target of peer ridicule and social prejudice and so, for their own good, should be taken from such an environment. In reply it is mentioned that this would be tantamount to saying that a child be removed from its white mother’s custody if she decided to marry a black man, for her children would be open to the same kind of ridicule.. In fact, such a case was dismissed in the US (Palmore vs Sidoti) and it was also “cited as a precedent in a 1985 Alaska decision, granting custody to a gay parent.”[66] For reasons, such as these, gay and lesbian liberationists suggest a case-by-case consideration in such matters, rather than a blanket ban.

My final critical comment on this issue is that, it seems to me, a child needs the nurturing love of partners of both sexes for it to grow into mature adulthood as also to find the necessary gender role models for life. Even if this situation is never provided perfectly, it doesn’t have to, as I have said. For an ideal to be experienced as relevant and appealing, it doesn’t have to always be encountered in its

---

64 Cf. R. Posner. 1992. *Sex and Reason,* Cambridge (US): Harvard University Press, p. 418 – quoted by Leahy and Sohn-Sherbok, *Op. cit.*, p. 103.

65 *Ibid.*

66 *Ibid.*

fullness amid the concrete realities of life. However a priori this may sound, I feel quite convinced that, viewing the normal unfolding of a child's psychological development, as well as that of the adolescent, only the context of a heterosexual family background does one find the best conditions for mature adult development. And I wouldn't be surprised if, when comprehensive data is finally forthcoming, they bear out the truth of my statement.

Conclusion

The Catechism of the Catholic Church has three paragraphs on homosexuality that merit being quoted in the full, even at the risk of some repetition:[67]

> Homosexuality refers to relations between men or between women who experience an exclusive or predominant sexual orientation towards persons of the same sex. It has taken a great variety of forms through the centuries and in different cultures. Its psychological genesis remains largely unexplained. Basing itself on Sacred Scripture, which presents homosexual acts as acts of grave depravity, tradition has always declared the "homosexual acts are intrinsically disordered". They are contrary to the natural law. They close the sexual act to the gift of life. They do not proceed from a genuine sexual complementarity. Under no circumstance can they be approved. (No. 2357)
>
> The number of men and women who have deep-seated homosexual tendencies is not negligible. They do not choose their homosexual tendencies; for most of them it is a trial. They must be treated, with respect, Compassion and sensitivity. Every sign of unjust discrimination in their regard should be avoided. These persons are called to fulfil God's will in their lives and, of they are Christians, to unite the Sacrifice of the Lord's Cross the difficulties they may encounter from their condition. (No. 2358),

67 *Op. cit. Catechism of the Catholic Church.*

> Homosexual persons are called-to chastity. By the virtues of self-mastery that teach them inner freedom, at times by the support of disinterested friendship, by prayer and sacramental grace, they can and should gradually and resolutely approach Christian perfection. (No. 2359)

It is indeed heartening to see such a balanced and sympathetic pastoral approach to this controversial and little-understood phenomenon. It must be admitted that this significant official Catholic response is far more human and understanding than that of many main-line religions and groups.

It is recognised that the homosexuality we are speaking of is not the result of a deliberate choice. Any oppression or discrimination against homosexually inclined persons is unequivocally condemned. Finally, it clearly rejects the popular prejudice that the homosexual is a totally depraved individual, impervious to noble values and incapable of any religious spiritual depth worthy of the name! They are not cursed by God and share in the universal human vocation to sainthood or perfection.

As for the passages in Sacred Scripture (The Bible) referred to in No. 2357,[68] it is not sure that the homosexuality condemned there is the kind of homosexuality we are talking about here (i.e. one not chosen by the persons themselves). Isn't it rather that sociological or cultural homosexuality, rampant at that, time, and still practised in Greece during the Golden Age of Socrates-Plato-Aristotle, deriving from an extreme male chauvinism, which so despised woman that it saw homosexuality as the only form of sexual love worthy of man, and which I have discussed earlier?

Many homosexuals revolt at being told that they are "unnatural" in this regard "My homosexuality and my left-handedness is as natural to me as your heterosexuality or your right-handedness seems natural to you!" a gay friend once told me. One cannot deny that homosexuals' lives and commitments of love (however authentic and loyal they may be) do lack a certain completeness and complementarity (discovery and celebration of the mystery of the

68 It may be noted that a footnote cites four of these: Gen 19:1-29. Rom l: 24-27, I Cor 6; 10 and I Tim 1; 10 – the last two being mere passing references.

opposite sex, sexually and otherwise, the production of children as the incarnation of the love experience of the couple, etc., detailed by me above and alluded to in No 2357).

I have expressed my reservations about the idea that a homosexual person is, *ipso facto,* as it were, "called to chastity". 1 have suggested however, that more study, reflection, empirical data (and prayer!) is required before we recommend as a "next-best-solution:" the possibility of a case-by-case decision as regards some kind of "homosexual marriage" but I don't see how adoption of children, or retaining their custody could be defended as in the best interests of the children themselves. It may require much more time and information to deal adequately with such a complex issue.

Some Quotes

"It's possible to love a human being if you don't know them too well."

– Charles Bukowski

"Never underestimate the capacity of another human being to have exactly the same shortcomings you have."

– Leigh Steinberg

"If you don't deal with your shadows, you are condemned to repeat the same mistake over and over, as a human being or as a society."

– Denis Villeneuve

"Man can never know the loneliness a woman knows. Man lies in the woman's womb only to gather strength, he nourishes himself from this fusion, and then he rises and goes into the world, into his work, into battle, into art. He is not lonely. He is busy. The memory of the swim in amniotic fluid gives him energy, completion. Woman may be busy too, but she feels empty. Sensuality for her is not only a wave of pleasure in which she is bathed, and a charge of electric joy at contact with another. When man lies in her womb, she is fulfilled, each act of love a taking of man within her, an act of birth and rebirth, of child rearing and man bearing. Man lies in her womb and is reborn each time anew with a desire to act, to be. But for woman, the climax is not in the birth, but in the moment man rests inside of her." – Anaïs Nin, *The Diary of Anaïs Nin*, Vol. 1: 1931-1934

Chapter 10

LIBERATIVE ANDROGOGICS

Introduction: Re-education

Action for justice and liberation entails enabling oppressed people to "deconstruct" the false awareness they had built up of themselves and the world, due to the very efficient brainwashing they had been submitted to by their oppressive situation. As a result of this, they had actually come to believe that they were sub-humans, radically inferior to the dominant classes (or castes!) and so deserve no better than to be exploited and then cast aside as old tools that have done their term of useful work. Indeed, they had come to accept that the set-up they were born into was either divinely intended or, somehow or the other, part of the very natural order of things. Hence, any attempt to question or change the status quo would be seen as a blasphemous revolt against God's "vast eternal plan" or a dangerous subversion of the cosmic order. As Ambedkar and other revolutionaries have realised, a necessary first step in liberating the oppressed is to re-educate them to open their eyes to this "false consciousness" that has been foisted upon them by vested interests who want the system to be maintained at all costs so that they could continue to derive profit, power and wealth from it ... at the expense of the oppressed. Only when such a movement has been inaugurated would the downtrodden be able to begin their demanding and difficult pilgrimage to realizing their status as authentic human subjects, on the way to becoming "fully human, fully alive" and no longer dependent on others to tell them who they are and what they should be and do in life.

From Pedagogics to Androgogics

Pedagogics is the term usually employed to designate the existing educational methods and techniques in a given set-up. Unfortunately, it is derived from the Greek word for a child (*pais, paidos*) and implies that the one to be educated is childish and immature and hence must be guided, led-in effect, told ("taught"?) what is good for him/her. Now it is quite common for (even well-meaning) would-be liberators of the oppressed to view the oppressed-whatever be their age-as children who need to be treated accordingly. Hence the revolutionary "leader" works out, with the people's alleged "best good" at heart, what their major problems are and how these are to be eradicated. The "leader" decides "for the people" what would be the most liberating worldview they must re-instate in place of the old oppressive one. Frequently the great leader will become impatient, irritated and angry with "the masses" who do not respond speedily enough and with sufficient gratitude to all that has been so painstakingly worked out for them. When (and if) the old regime is overthrown, it cannot but be the revolutionary leader who must assume command and jealously guard the reins of power: after all, who but he (it is invariably a "he"!) knows what's best for the ignorant, childish masses, who would never be able to take charge of themselves. Invariably, in spite of the (probable?) good intentions of the would-be liberator of the masses, the "revolution" brings about for the oppressed but a "change of dictatorships".

In course of time, the "benevolence" of the "leader" begins to wear down and rapidly becomes ruthlessness, as all slowness and hesitation on the part of the people is interpreted as opposition to the "New Order" and the apparent foot-dragging of the people is dealt with swiftly, efficiently and cruelly: "these stupid people don't even know what's to their own good!" Thus, the "second state is soon worse than the first"! How many histories of national upheaval and dissidence have been variations of this theme!

Androgogics is a relatively new term and is acquiring prominence in discussions of Liberative education. It comes from the Greek word for an adult (*aner, andros*) and implies recognising that the one to be educated (whether literate or not) is a mature, critical person. Hence, the approach of the would-be educator-revolutionary is not to tell or teach the people what their situation is, and how it should be remedied. Rather such a person's goal would be to facilitate their growth in awareness of the actual state of affairs, enabling them to discover for themselves that there is nothing natural, divine, mysterious or magical about their set-up. On the contrary, it must be shown up for what it is: an artificial construct of vested interests who know that their security, power and wealth would be jeopardised by any challenge to the status quo. It's not a mere matter of "telling" the people all this': rather, is it a question of dialoguing with them, critical reflection, bringing about a true re-education and and empowerment of the people. The implicit assumption is that only the oppressed can liberate both themselves and their'oppressors. The revolutionary leader-cum-educator has the responsibility to work *with*, never merely *for*, the people.

Now perhaps no one is better qualified to initiate us into the theory and practice of such liberative education (a regular "cultural revolution", if ever there was one) as the Brazilian activist, Paulo Freire. His involvement in the "conscientisation" of broken people all over the world, especially in Latin America, has won international acclaim and offers us quite a few provocative and disturbing insights.

Paulo Freire: Twentieth Century Luminary

With the dawn of the so-called Third Millennium, very many people have attempted to draw up "lists" of leading lights of the Century, if not the Millennium itself. Various candidates have been proposed and the debate rages fierce and free as to whose life and achievement has been most inspiring for the most number of people and in the largest number of fields. I have noticed many men (and some women) of the realms of the Arts and Sciences coming up for mention: mainly people whose lives and achievement have made life more secure, comfortable or pleasant to the upper-middle-class and above. Not many times are names like Helder Camara, Ambedkar, Rani Maria and Oscar Romero been proposed. Apparently the "little one's" whose lives and freedom they have enhanced were too little to be noticed, no matter how many they may be, nor how momentous a change in their lifestyles these luminaries had effected. Whatever, my vote for luminary of the century would be for Paulo Freire, whose theory and praxis have not only been an inspiration to millions of depressed and dehumanized people all over the world, but have also opened the eyes of many would-be revolutionaries to recognize that their way of proceeding was not really liberating the oppressed, however well-meaning and nobly-intentioned such activists may have been in their approach.

Paulo Freire was a Brazilian, born 1921 in Recife, the largest metropolitan area in Brazil, later to become famous as the diocese of Dom Helder Camara, whose commitment to the oppressed natives of this, one of the most impoverished regions of the world, long pre-dated the Theology of Liberation Movement. Little Paulo grew up in a fairly well-to-do middle class family but a sudden reverse in fortunes put an end to what might have been a life of quiet ease and comfort.

In 1929, there was the famous Stock Market Crash in the US, followed by the Great Depression whose disastrous consequences were felt far beyond the borders of the United States ... and, naturally, many Latin American nations were the hardest hit. The Freire family was affected and, by 1932, 11 year old Paulo began to experience first-hand the physical and psychological toll of poverty. Gnawing hunger made him listless and, unable to concentrate on his studies, he fell back in school. The worst was over by the time he was out of his teens, but the harrowing experience had left an indelible mark on the growing lad. He vowed to wage a relentless war against hunger and poverty, so that no other children be forced to go through the terrible ordeal he had to suffer in his own tender years. Thus, the tools of his *Pedagogy of the Oppressed* were forged in the crucible of his own suffering. He pin-pointed the Culture of Silence which such misery elicited: the fact that the poor were imprisoned and mired in a whole complexus of ignorance and helpessness that they felt totally submerged. This resulted in a spirit of such lethargy and powerlessness that all critique and response from their part was rendered ineffective.

Paulo Freire secured his Ph.D in Education from the University of Recife, in 1959, drawing upon the radical insights of such a wide gallery of epoch-making thinkers as Sartre, Mounier, Fromm, Althusser, Ortega Y. Gasset, Marx and Mao. While he worked as Professor of the History of Education at his alma mater, Catholic Social Activists and other committed persons were making enthusiastic use of his revolutionary androgogics, with his full approval.

Then there came the military coup of 1964 and the Brazilian Generals found Frere's views too threatening to the established order (which they wished to maintain), so they had him arrested. Imprisoned for 70 days, he was only released when he agreed to go into exile. Then followed a long stint of work with the UNESCO and various Adult Education Programmes, in collaboration with the WCC all over Latin America and Africa. Invitations poured in for him to lecture and give advice everywhere.

Pedagogy of the Oppressed, whom many hail as his masterpiece, came out, in both the original Portuguese, as well as an English translation, in 1967. By 1970 when *Cultural Action for Freedom* saw the light of day, conscientisation and other Freirean terminology become household words.

In a short span of time, Paulo Freire's ideas had spread all over Latin America and struck a responsive chord in the hearts of all oppressed people, everywhere in Africa and Asia, as people long kept ignorant and unaware of their inherent dignity and right to freedom began to awaken after a long darkness and sought a liberative praxis to guide their faltering steps on the long march to liberation and nationhood. Nowadays, even middle-class youth in the US and Europe are finding inspiration in his vision. Truly, Paulo Freire is the relevant twentieth century thinker for the Philosophy of Liberation.

PAULO FREIRE'S KEY IDEAS

Hope for the Oppressed

The "Dedication" of his *Pedagogy of the Oppressed*[69] reads, "To the Oppressed, and to those who suffer with them, and fight by their side". The choice of the phrases "with", and "by their side"-and not merely "for" is significant. For Freire, the authentic revolutionary works, fights and suffers with the oppressed and by their side, not from a relatively more comfortable and secure command post somewhere in the rear. Nor can one be a true revolutionary if one has not, for an appreciable time, seen known and lived, first-hand, the plight of the people.

Paulo Freire reinstates the humanizing and liberative vocation of the intellectual, as against the sterile academics so prevalent in First World Universities. Radical thoughts must be geared to creative action for justice, they must open out new, hopeful visions of freedom and map out a route to get there!

Above all, no matter how "ignorant" or "helpless" a peasant may be-either in his own eyes or those of others-he/she is capable of critical reflection and can elaborate a wholly new vision of reality with a little help through "dialogical education". Peasants can, without too much difficulty, regain their awareness as subjects, as agents who can act on, and transform, their world, not just be fashioned by it. They gradually realize that the "world" is not a static "given" (by God or by "nature") to which they must accommodate themselves. The present "order" and the suffering and misery it brings them, far from being ultimate or inevitable, is an artificial construct made by vested interests: it can be radically transformed! To effect this transformation, one must make use of the technological development of the West, but, at the same time draw upon the more personal, social vision of the Third World. Above all, it is a fellow peasant, rather than a teacher from outside, who can best effect the process of critical awareness through dialogical encounter. "Men educate each other through a mediation

69 Paulo Freire. 1972. *Pedagogy of the Oppressed.* trsl. Myra Ramos, Penguins, Hammondsworth.

of the world."[70] Indeed, *it is only the oppressed who can liberate both themselves and their oppressors, both of whom have been dehumanized by the oppressive situation.*

Thus, "the word" no longer remains something fearful, magical or abstract for the illiterate: it takes on a new power in human hands and enables human persons to recover a lost potential, the ability to "say one's own word, to name the world" (Ibid). From this arises a new self-awareness in the peasant, a new feeling of self-worth (conscientisation), whereby the peasant can create a whole new culture: "I work, and working, I transform the world!"

The "Fear of Freedom"

The oppressive class, in whose favour the unjust situation subsists, naturally fear any attempt to question, let alone subvert, the established "order". However, very cleverly, they pose as "defenders freedom" and try to argue that any attempt to conscientise the people or make them aware of their dignity and rights would lead to chaos, violence and anarchy. The people, they maintain, are immature and naive: they wouldn't be able to handle freedom: they are really "happier this way", resigned to their lot. Freire shows that critical consciousness removes both fear and feelings of helplessness from the people. The fallacy is that people in power tend to "confuse freedom with the maintenance of the status quo: so if conscientisation threatens to place that status quo in question, it thereby seems to constitute a threat to freedom itself."[71] We must distinguish between authentic radicalism, founded on the human ontological vocation to be an active responsible subjects and sectarianism "fed by fanaticism" which "is always castrating". Authentic conscientisation enables human persons to enter "the historical process as subjects", it "enrolls them in the search for self-affirmation", which destroys all possibilities of fanaticism and destructiveness".

Now, there is both a sectarianism of the Right (the Christian variety) and a sectarianism of the Left (the Marxist variety). The former "wants to slow down the historical process to domesticate'

70 *Pedagogy*, p. 12.

71 *Ibid.* p. 16.

time and thus to domesticate man."[72] The Leftist-turned-sectarian goes astray inasmuch as he "attempts to interpret reality and history dialectically, and falls into fatalistic temptations."[73] Such a sectarian doesn't take human subject hood seriously. In passing, we may note that Freire's usage of terms like "the Rightist-turned-sectarian" and "the leftist-turned-sectarian" obviously implies that he doesn't think that the Christian must necessarily be a sectarian any more than he would hold that all Marxists cannot but end up as sectarian in outlook!

> The Rightist sectarian differs from his Leftist counterpart in that the former attempts to deomesticate the present so that (he hopes) the future will reproduce the domesticated present, while the latter considers the future pre-established-a kind of inevitable fate, fortune or destiny. For the Rightist sectarian, "today" linked to the past, is something given and immutable; for the Leftist sectarian, "tomorrow" is decreed beforehand, is inextricably foreordained. This Rightist and this Leftist are both reactionary because, starting from their respective false views of history, both develop forms of action which negate freedom.[74]

The Universal Call to Humanization

As history shows us, both "humanization" and "dehumanization" are possibilities open to men and women today as historical possibilities, though (obviously!) only humanization can be hailed as our authentic "vocation". However, there are people who seemed determined to ensure that some human beings will never achieve this goal and do all they can to prevent it. Dehumanization, then, marks both the oppressed and the oppressor and marks them off as "those whose humanity has been stolen" and "those who have stolen it". But if dehumanization is "a concrete historical fact", it cannot be seen as our "given destiny": it is the result of an unjust social

72 *Pedagogy*, p. 17.

73 *Ibid.*, p. 18.

74 *Ibid.*, p. 9.

order which has been violently foisted upon the oppressed by the oppressor. Eventually the oppressors will, as it were, push their luck too far and the long-suffering and resigned victims of oppression will be provoked to struggle against those who have dehumanized them. However, in the process of this revolt, "the oppressed must not, in seeking to regain their humanity ... become oppressors of the oppressors", for then they will once again dehumanise themselves. The oppressor, by one and the same act, dehumanizes both himself and those he oppresses. Rather, the oppressed must seek to become-as only they can-"restorers of the humanity of both."[75]

> This then is the great humanistic and historical task of the oppressed: to liberate themselves and their oppressors as well. The oppressors, who oppress, exploit and rape by virtue of their power, cannot find in this power the strength to liberate the oppressed or themselves. Only power that springs from the weakness of the oppressed will be sufficiently strong to free both.[76]

False Generosity and False Models

In order to defuse a potentially revolutionary situation, the oppressor tries to assuage the anger of the oppressed and contain their revolutionary action by "false generosity". Wages will be raised a little (but still be kept at an unjustly low level), violence against the "masses" will be mitigated somewhat (but not completely), unfair demands will continue-but be reduced somewhat ... and, very often, they succeed in fooling the "revolutionary leaders" who rejoice at the "respite" they have "won". And the protests are called off. However, "true generosity" would seek to "destroy the causes which nourish false charity", whereas the latter wants "the fearful and subdued" to continue to "extend their trembling hands" in suppliant plea.

Now there is an extremely vicious and powerful "block" to the oppressed people's action for justice. Aside from external obstacles (such as the risks entailed in the dangerous enterprise and the fact

75 *Pedagogy*, p. 21.

76 *Ibid.*

that a possible failure would provoke a backlash against them by their fellows, who fear greater repression in the aftermath of the scuttled attempt) there is the internal block! This consists of the ominous internalized contradiction that the subjugated people are living out: their nigh unconscious identification with the oppressor! This is one of Freire's most insightful observations and can help us understand much of the complex psychology of the "wretched of the earth".

To break out of this paralyzing condition implies, first of all, overcoming "the duality which has been established in their innermost being."[77]

> They discover that without freedom they cannot exist authentically. Yet, although they desire authentic existence', they fear it. They are, at one and the same time, themselves and the oppressor whose consciousness they have internalized. The conflict lies in the choice between being wholly themselves or being divided; between ejecting the oppressor within or not ejecting him; between human solidarity or alienation; between following prescriptions or making choices; between being spectators or actors; between speaking out or being silent, castrated in their power to Create and recreate, in their power to transform the world. This is the tragic dilemma of the oppressed which their education must take into account.[78]

But why do the oppressed "internalize" the image of their oppressor at all? For the simple reason that, after having undergone long periods (centuries?) of oppression, they have become brain-washed into seeing the oppressor solely as human. He is thus, their role model in their quest for humanization. For the oppressed, "to be is to be like, and to be like is to be like the oppressor."[79]

Perhaps now we can understand why so many Dalits and Adivasis, when given positions of power, as per the "reservation quota" (in the Police Force or Customs) act so rude and arrogant. This is the

77 *Pedagogy*, p. 12.

78 *Ibid.*, pp. 24-25.

79 *Ibid.*

only way to wield power that they know of. So, when they attain some important posts they "lord it over others"-not so much "out of revenge" as some think, but because this is how they have seen their role models exercising authority. They know no other way to show their pre-eminence and in order to demonstrate that they can do the authority job as well as those they have observed, they act just like them, treating others as they have been treated!

Something like this is at play when oppressed people turn against each other in acts of horrifying and unbridled violence-which leads the oppressors to be confirmed in their opinion that "the niggers" are uncivilized barbarians and need only the stick and the whip to make them behave. After all, 'If that's the way they treat each other, what can we, their betters, expect at their hands if they were given freedom?' And Freire quotes, with agreement, the chilling comment of Franz Fannon:

> The colonized man will first manifest this aggressiveness, which has been deposited in his bone's, against his own people. This is the period when the niggers beat each other up, and the police and the magistrates don't know which way to turn when faced with the astonishing waves of crime in North Africa. ... While the settler or the policeman has the right the livelong day to strike the native, to insult him and to make him crawl to them, you will see the native reaching for his knife at the slightest hostile or aggressive glance cast on him by another native; for the last resort of the native is to defend his personality vis-a-vis his brother.[80]

For the oppressed, then, the oppressor alone is truly human and, as such, he is an oppressor. Hence, the oppressed believe that their only possibility of becoming "humanized" is to become oppressors. So, instead of striving to liberate themselves from the yoke of the oppressor, they seek every occasion to become oppressors or "sub-oppressors", laying down the law with cruel severity for their subordinates, helpless women, little children and those weaker than themselves.

---

80 Franz Fannon, *The Wretched of the Earth*, quoted in *Pedagogy*, p. 38.

Solidarity

It is interesting to note that Paulo Freire sets great store by "solidarity", a word that we all associate with the liberation of nations who had been groaning under the thrall of the Russian bear: Lech Walesa, the former dockworker of Gdaansk, used that as the name of his defiant Trade Union, which sparked off a series of minor revolts that ultimately climaxed in the collapse of the Iron Curtain, starting with the Fall of the Berlin Wall in 1989. As Freire puts it,

> If what characterizes the oppressed is their subordination to the consciousness of the master, as Hegel affairs, true solidarity with the oppressed means fighting at their side to transform the objective reality which has made them these "beings for another". The oppressor shows solidarity with the oppressed only when he stops regarding the oppressed as an abstract category and sees them as persons who have been unjustly dealt with, deprived of their voice, cheated in the sale of their labour-when he stops making pious, sentimental and individualistic gestures and risks an act of love. True solidarity is found only in the plenitude of this act of love, in its existentiality, in its praxis. It is a farce to affirm that men are people and thus should be free, yet do nothing tangible to make this affirmation a reality.[81]

Subjectivity and Objectivity; Praxis

Liberation, Freire reminds us, is a kind of childbirth and, like all childbirths, is a painful process. It can only happen when a new person is born into the world, one who is "no longer oppressor or oppressed, but ... in the process of achieving freedom."[82] This "painful process" as we have called it, comprises an objective as well as a subjective element.

As regards the objective dimension, it is required that the oppressed be able to perceive their situation as it really is: an oppressive, limiting situation which is not inescapable and immutable, but one which

81 Franz Fannon, *The Wretched of the Earth*, quoted in *Pedagogy*, p. 26.

82 *Ibid.*, p. 25.

they can transform. But this must imply that they recognize that it is they, as free and conscious subjects, who must make the change. There is no place for what Freire calls "subjectivist immobility", i.e. a passive and patient waiting for the oppressor to disappear by himself. In other words, what is needed is authentic praxis. that is, reflection and action on the world to transform it. But this cannot be built upon a false perception of reality; the' oppressed must "confront ...reality critically, simultaneously objectifying and acting upon that reality."[83]

As Jose Luis Fiori tellingly observes, a true perception of an oppressive situation makes "real oppression more oppressive by adding to it the realization of oppression". This is the truth that makes one mad and provokes action for justice and freedom.

Liberative Education

This true perception of the oppressive situation, coupled with inspiration for critical intervention, obviously involves liberative education. Let us not forget that the oppressor will try his best to convince the people that any intervention would not be to their best interests-actually, he knows full well that disturbing the status quo would not be to his vested interests. So he, cleverly, assumes the pose of one who only seeks the good of those he's oppressing!

Such liberative education can hardly be carried out by a systematic new education policy, for that requires political power to implement it. However, educational projects can be launched. This doesn't presuppose possession of political power but action with the oppressed, organizing and conscientising them.

Now, one can distinguish as many as two phases in this markedly humanistic and liberative style of education. First, the oppressed unveil and discover their situation of oppression, recognizing that there is nothing magical or divine or natural about it. They critically confront the understanding of the world that they have been given and which they have received. Then, as a group, they must commit themselves, through praxis, to transform it. The second phase is equally important: this begins when the above situation has been

---

83 Franz Fannon, *The Wretched of the Earth*, quoted in *Pedagogy*, p. 28.

transformed. This involves a veritable cultural revolution, wherein old myths must be discarded and new, liberative, goals and values are introduced. Both stages call for in-depth reflection and action, by means of which the old culture of domination is confronted, ousted and replaced by a new liberative culture. "Never in history has violence been initiated by the oppressed", Freire observes: rather, they are its products:

> Any situation in which A objectively exploits B or hinders his pursuit of self-affirmation as a responsible person is one of oppression. Such a situation itself constitutes violence, even when sweetened by false generosity, because it interferes with man's ontological and historical vocation to be fully human. With the establishment of a relationship of oppression, violence has already begun.[84]

We recall Dom Helder Camara's depiction of three types of violence, in his masterly and insightful study *Spiral of Violence*. There is first structural violence or institutional violence: this is the one that Freire has just described and would comprise oppressive set-ups like apartheid, the caste system or any form of discrimination which is "incarnate" in a particular socio-cultural situation and thereby deprives some persons of full development because of their gender, ethnicity or some such criterion. Then there comes insurrectional violence in which the people, driven to desperation by the rape and pillage they have been systematically subject to, "hit back" at their oppressors, through riots and civil disturbances. Finally, there is repressive violence whereby the State feels justified in calling in the Army, heavy artillery and whatnot to put down, with brutal means, the protests of the people. As a result, a new stricture of violence is institutionalized, more terrible than the first. For example, under the guide of "Anti-Terrorism Laws", basic human rights such as freedom of speech and assembly-even of movement-are restricted (allegedly for a while): people can be arrested and detained without warrant for unspecified periods of time and so on. Eventually this new oppressive situation becomes so unbearable that it provokes the people to a

84 Franz Fannon, *The Wretched of the Earth*, quoted in *Pedagogy*, p. 31.

fresh outbreak of violence and this, in turn, unleashes more waves of police brutality ... and the cycle of violence spirals on and on.

Significantly, as Helder Camara remarks, only the second instance of violence is called such. The unjust situation which kept people in subjection, is not perceived as violent, however much it may destroy, cripple and maim people in their quest for humanness and fullness of life. As for the last mentioned, however brutal and ruthless it may be, that is covered over with the euphemism of "restoring order" (when, in reality, it is but seeking to restore the established disorder!). It is only the desperate reaction of the people to all the injustices and dehumanization they have so long suffered that is hailed as "violence". It is commonly held that, in so doing, the people have "created violence", implying that it never existed before! Popular parlance and uncritical sociologies are highly selective in their phenomenology and hermeneutics.

> Violence is initiated by those who oppress, who exploit, who fail to recognize others as people-not by those who are oppressed, exploited and unrecognized. It is not the unloved who cause disaffection, but those who cannot love because they love only themselves. It is not the helpless, subject to terror, who initiate terror, but the violent, who, with their power: 'create the concrete situation which begets 'the rejects of life'. It is not the tyrannized who are the sources of despotism , but the tyrants; not the despised who initiate hatred, but those who despise them. It is not those whose humanity is denied them who negate man, but those who denied that humanity (thus negating their own, as well). Force is not used by those who have become weak under the preponderance of the strong, but by the strong who have emasculated them.[85]

The oppressors, after all, are the sole one's in charge of words and names. It is the oppressor who label the oppressed "those people", "the masses", "savages", "natives". And when the latter react in desperation,

85 Franz Fannon, *The Wretched of the Earth,* quoted in *Pedagogy*, p. 32.

having been pushed beyond all reasonable limits, it is the oppressors who brand them as "violent", "uncivilized", "uncultured", etc.

Indeed, Freire is totally at variance with Gandhi as regards the use of violence by the oppressed and the oppressor. Whereas the Mahatma condemned all violence, no matter what be its occasion and context, as a crime against humanity, the Brazilian activist sees the cruel acts of the oppressor and the revolutionary action and protest of the oppressed as two qualitatively different actions. Paradoxically enough, in Freire's view, the violence of the oppressed, in resisting the violence of the oppressor, contains "a gesture of love". Even though the act of rebellion of the oppressed may be "as violent as the initial violence of the oppressors", it can "initiate love"!

This is because the oppressors' violence, "prevents the oppressed from being fully human" and, inasmuch as it dehumanizes others, it also dehumanizes the perpetrator. On the contrary, the response of the oppressed to this, violent though it be in itself, "is grounded in the desire to pursue the right to be human", while the violence of the oppressor denies this same right. But "the oppressed, fighting to be human, take away the oppressors' power to dominate" and, by doing so, not only restore their own humanity, but also restore that of their oppressors. That is why "only the oppressed ... by freeing themselves can free their oppressors."[86]

> The latter, as an oppressive class, can neither free others nor themselves. It is therefore essential that the oppressed wage the struggle to resolve the contradiction in which they are caught. That contradiction will be resolved by the appearance of the new man who is neither oppressor nor oppressed-man in the process of liberation. If the goal of the oppressed is to become fully human, they will not achieve their goal by merely reversing the terms of the contradiction, by simply changing poles.[87]

Nor can we simplistically label as "oppression" the restrictions that the formerly oppressed people put on their ex-oppressors so as

86 Franz Fannon, *The Wretched of the Earth*, quoted in *Pedagogy*, pp. 31-32.

87 *Ibid.*, pp. 32-33.

to prevent them from regaining their old oppressive positions and powers. For "(a)n act is oppressive only when it prevents men from being more fully human . . . These "necessary restraints do not in themselves signify that yesterday s oppressed have become today's oppressors."[88]

But this always remains a real and dangerous possibility. It is all too easy for the former oppressed to degenerate into the new oppressor class and wreak fearful and oppressive vengeance on the old oppressors. If "the new regime hardens into a dominating 'bureaucracy'", then the humanistic dimension is lost and liberation is also forfeited. Of course, the oppressor will not at all feel liberated or humanized, even in the context of an authentic, humanizing liberative set-up. For he experiences as oppression any situation in which he cannot live as he lived before-even if it was built on a system that simply denied to others the right to live humanly.

> Formerly, they could eat, dress, wear shoes, be educated, travel and hear Beethoven; while millions did not eat, had no clothes or shoes, neither studied nor travelled, much less listened to Beethoven. Any restriction on this way of life, in the name of the rights of the community, appears to the former oppressors as a profound violation of their individual rights-although they had no respect for the millions who suffered and died of hunger, pain, sorrow and despair. For the oppressors, 'human beings' refers only to themselves; other people are 'things'. For the oppressors there exists only one right: their right to live in peace, over and against the right, not always even recognized, but merely conceded, of the oppressed to survival. (*Ibid.*, p. 34)
>
> And they make this concession only because the existence of the oppressed is necessary to their own existence.

88 Franz Fannon, *The Wretched of the Earth*, quoted in *Pedagogy*, p. 33.

The Oppressors 'Necrophilia'

The tendency of the oppressors to build their happiness on the suffering and dehumanization of the oppressed is nothing less than a "tendency to sadism", as Freire notes that Fromm had observed:

> The pleasure in complete domination over another person (or other animate creature) is the very essence of the sadistic drive. Another way of formulating the same thought is to say that the aim of sadism is to transform a man into a thing, something 'animate into something inanimate, since by complete and absolute control, the living loses one essential quality of life – freedom.[89]

Consequently, the only kind of love that the oppressor can know is a perverted kind of love, a love of death, not life. The oppressor's consciousness is thereby necrophilia (Greek, *nekros* = death). That is why the oppressor has no hesitation to use the latest "state of the art" technology for the sole purpose of elaborating better and more efficient means to maintain the oppressive set-up.

The Demystification of the Oppressor

Centuries of oppression have gradually built into the oppressed the idea that that their overlords are some kind of super-human, invincible and invulnerable beings. Thus the latter alone can be said "to be;" as for themselves, their way of being is "to be under" and to be under means to be under their oppressors. As long as the peasant, for instance, lives in a state of emotional dependence on the oppressor, will his own behaviour also be necrophilia, destructive of life. -

> It is only when the oppressed find the oppressor out and become involved in the organized struggle for their liberation that they begin to believe in themselves. This discovery cannot be purely intellectual, but must involve action; nor can it be limited to mere activism, but must include serious ref-lection: only then will it be a praxis.[90]

89 Franz Fannon, *The Wretched of the Earth*, quoted in *Pedagogy*, p. 36.

90 *Ibid.*, pp. 40-41.

It is only the path of reflection-action-reflection that can deconstruct the false understanding of the oppressor that reduces the oppressed majority to a state of abject, grovelling dependence. Once this "mystique" of the all-powerful, irresistible and undethronable oppressor is demystified can the oppressed begin to take steps towards authentic humanization.

The Call for Praxis

Critical and liberative dialogue presupposes action and has to be carried on at every stage of the struggle for liberation. This is true praxis. The action-reflection dialectic must always be there: the proportions and content may vary, due to historical conditions and the level at which the oppressed are able to perceive reality. The reflection must be built on authentic dialogue, not monologue, harangues, communiqués or slogans: these latter are instruments of domestication, not liberation. The participation of the people in the process is crucial: neglecting this vital dimension would be tantamount to treating, the people as "objects to be saved from a burning building"![91] It is essential that at every stage of the revolution the oppressed be, and see themselves to be, people engaged in the ontological and historical struggle to fulfil their vocation to be fully human and fully alive. Nor will a mere "armchair revolution" suffice: true reflection leads to action and authentic action requires its consequences to be critically analyzed: this is praxis!

> In this sense, praxis is the new raison d'etre of the oppressed; and the revolution, which inaugurates the historical moment of this raison d'etre is not viable apart from their concomitant conscious involvement. Otherwise, action is pure activism.[92]

All this calls for a genuine trust by the would-be revolutionary leader(s) in the oppressed and their ability to reason and to act. Praxis must be truly pedagogical action with the oppressed. Authentic revolutionary leaders must eschew any semblance of taking advantage of the oppressed people's emotional dependence.

91 Franz Fannon, *The Wretched of the Earth*, quoted in *Pedagogy*, p. 41.

92 *Ibid.*

In the last analysis no leader-even the best intentioned-can *give* freedom or independence to people, for these are not things but persons. By that same token, it can be attained only by humans: "it cannot be achieved by semi-humans"[93]: the job of the leader is to facilitate the process by means of which the people realize and re-discover their essential humanness, which centuries of oppression has denied them and convinced them that they lack. Nor can this be attained by mere propaganda, revolutionary pep-talks! Only dialogue can bring about this conscientisation. As we have said before, leaders must carry out a revolution with the people (experiencing their lot and struggling side by side with them): there is no such thing as revolutionary action merely for the people, not with them!

Liberative Education

Many would-be revolutionary leaders, impatient for results, try to "implant" a belief in freedom and independence in the oppressed peoples' hearts and minds and hurry them along in the process of humanization. In doing so, however, one is-like the oppressor!-treating them as things. But the oppressed "cannot enter the struggle as objects in order, later to become human".[94]

Mere propaganda is not "pedagogy of the oppressed", much less is it true andragogy. At most, it might give oppressed people temporary liberation from hunger and the people must needs be liberated from other oppressions, too. Fromm lists some of these:

> ... Freedom to create and construct, to wander and to venture, such freedom requires that the individual be active and responsible, not a slave or a well-fed cog in a machine. ... It is not enough that men are not slaves; if social conditions further the existence of automatons, the result will not be love of life, but love of death.[95]

All this is to be achieved, not by having traditional teachers using the people as students, but by "co-intentional education", the

93 Franz Fannon, *The Wretched of the Earth*, quoted in *Pedagogy*, p. 42

94 *Ibid.*, p. 44). Actually Freire had written "men" instead of "humans"!

95 Erich Fromm, *The Heart of Man*, cited by Freire, *Pedagogy*, p. 43.

only form of liberative education. Here, both teachers (leaders) and students (the people) are subjects as regards the discovery, unveiling, critiquing and re-creating of reality. Gone is the old water-tight distinction between the purely active teacher and the purely passive students: there is the student-teacher and the teacher-students. Both teach each other, both learn together.

The Traditional "Banking System" of Education

Paulo Freire's felicitous phrase neatly sums up the method-and deficiency-of traditional-education: it is a "banking system". In the first place, it is of a fundamentally narrative nature, whereby the teacher is the sole active and narrating subject, the students are seen as, and required to be, passive, listening objects and the contents of the narrative (values, empirical reality, etc.) are, in the process, rendered lifeless and petrified. Secondly, its methodology is unabashedly that of banking. The teacher talks about reality as if it were motionless, static and compartmentalized or else discourses on issues totally alien to the students' experience. The teacher's goal is to "deposit" his knowledge, by means of words that are hollow, alienated and alienating, in the "minds" of the students. The latter's role is limited to being good containers: the more passively, meekly and obediently they function as these "vaults of the teachers' wisdom", to be returned faithfully to them on demand (at examination time), the better student-containers they are the higher will they be graded.

Now this is a very oppressive understanding of education. Among other things, it sees the teacher as possessing absolute intelligence, while the student is attributed with absolute ignorance. Indeed, it is only, and as long as, they accept their ignorance that they justify the teachers' existence: that is why teachers see any assertion of the students' intelligence (such as questioning the formers' views) as a threat to their own status and a subversion of the proper order.

As a matter of fact, the "banking system of education" is founded on certain presuppositions that characterize all oppressive set-ups as a whole! It implies two parties and invests each with qualities such that it is inevitable that one emerges as the oppressor and the other as the oppressed. One is active, the other is passive; one is seen as all-knowing, the other as ignorant; one alone thinks, the other is "thought about;" one metes out discipline according to his whims and fancies, the other is disciplined and has little hope in a court of appeal; one chooses and enforces his choices; the other must accept the former's choices; one elaborates his programme without consulting the other, the other must accept the former's choices blindly; one confuses the authority of his knowledge with the authority of his profession and sees the freedom of others as a challenge to his position in the status quo; the other accepts this view-or is obliged to, under pain of severe penalties.

'From "Necrophily" to "Biophily"

The banking system of education reduces persons to the status of adaptable, manageable things. It kills the creative and critical sense of the student, on which our very humanness is rooted. As Simone de Beauvoir, quoted by Freire[96] notes, the banking-clerk-teacher seeks to change "the consciousness of the oppressed, not the situation which oppresses them": in effect such an educational system aims at convincing the suffering and dispossessed that what is happening is the best for them and any attempt to subvert the set-up would be a relapse into anarchy, barbarism and license. In short, this is an approach ground on a love of death or Necrophily, not a love of life or Biophily, in Fromm's felicitous phrase.

> Education must begin with the solution of the teacher-student contradiction, by reconciling the poles of the contradiction so that both are simultaneously teachers and students.[97]

Authentic education is founded on true communication and dialogue, not 'deposits' and 'communiques' foisted by the teacher on the hapless students.

> The teacher's thinking is authenticated only by the authenticity of the students' thinking. The teacher cannot think for his students, nor can he impose his thought on

96 *Pedagogy*, p. 46.

97 *Ibid.* p. 52.

> them. Authentic thinking, thinking that is concerned about reality, does not take place in ivory-tower isolation, but only in communication. If it is true that thought has meaning only when it is generated by action upon the world, the subordination of students to teachers becomes impossible. (Ib.. p. 50)[98]

Oppression, inasmuch as it is "overwhelming control" is unavoidably necrophilic and the banking system of education, which serves the interests of oppression, is also necrophilic.

> The necrophilous person can relate to an object-a flower or a person-only if he possesses it; hence a threat to his possession is a threat to himself; if he loses possession he loses contact with the world. ... He loves control, and in the act of controlling he kills life.[99]

'Problem-Posing' or 'Dialogical' Education

This form of education "responds to the essence of consciousness"–intentionality-and "embodies (authentic) communication". It breaks down the watertight distinctions of students and teacher (or "teacher-of-the-students" and "students-of-the-teacher", to be precise) and replaces them with new partners, the teacher-student and the students-teacher. The teacher is no longer merely the-one-who-teaches but one-who-is-also-taught in dialogue with the students, who also teach. True authority "must be on the side of freedom, not against it."[100] Here, no one merely teaches and none is self-taught. Both teach each other, mediated by the world, rather than one ("the teacher") who owns the cognisable objects he/she serves up to the students.

The banking system distinguishes two clear stages in the teacher's role, adding yet another dichotomy to the whole process). First the teacher "cognizes" the object as he prepares his class, isolated in his laboratory. Then he expounds his cognition of the object to the

98 *Pedagogy*, p. 50.

99 Quoted from Fromm's *Heart of Man* in Freire, *Pedagogy*, p. 51.

100 *Ibid.*

students. The latter are required but to memorise what the teacher has narrated. They are deprived of all direct cognition with the cognisable object, which remains the private property of the teacher. Thus, in the name of preservation of culture and knowledge we have a system which achieves neither true knowledge nor true culture!

In problem-posing education the traditional dichotomies are avoided. The teacher-student is not seen, at first, as purely cognitive (while preparing his class) and then narrative (when "teaching it" to his students). Teacher and students are both cognitive throughout the process, in dialogue. The teacher doesn't usurp possession of the "cognisable object" which is "sealed off", as it were, from the student. Both of them approach the living, breathing cosmos as their common medium of reflection and critical analysis, each contributing to create knowledge as logos superseding it as mere *doxa* (the canonization of what is, in the last analysis, merely the teacher's opinion).

> Whereas banking education anaesthetises and inhibits creative power, problem-posing education involves a constant unveiling of reality. The former attempts to maintain the submersion of consciousness; the latter strives for the emergence of consciousness and critical intervention in reality.[101]

Now, perhaps, we can understand why Paulo Freire characterises problem-posing or dialogical education as the practice of freedom", in contrast with "banking education" as "the practice of domination."[102] Now, the basic difference between the two approaches consists in the fact that the latter seems to think that the human person and the world exist in isolation from each other, whereas the former asserts their interdependent existence. There is no human person apart from the world: as Rahner would say, we are Spirit in the World-our "being-in-the-world" as much a necessary constituent of our make-up as is our body. Nor would there be, strictly speaking, a world if there were no human person to say, "This is a world!" Consciousness

101 *Pedagogy*, p. 54.

102 *Ibid.*

and the world are simultaneous: one neither precedes nor follows the other.

Furthermore, problem-posing education sees the world not as a static reality, but in the process of development and transformation. As we gaze upon the world different aspects tend "to stand out" as we shift our attention or perspective ever so slightly. What "stands out" then assumes the character of a problem that calls -for deeper reflection

De-Mythicising

Banking education, as it is in favour of maintaining the status quo (which is exactly what the oppressor class, with its vested interests wants), sees the present set-up as something to be conserved at all costs and sets about trying to "mythicise" it: in other words, it seeks all manner of pseudo-scientific or bogus theologico-philosophical explanations as to why things have been so organized and why they must be left so. Problem-posing education, through dialogue, aims at critical cognition whereby the students are enabled to have an alternative vision of reality, as false concepts, naming and interpretations are unmasked or unveiled. Dialogical education looks upon students as critical thinkers and calls upon creativity, stimulating true reflection and action on reality.

In sum: "banking theory and practice, as immobilizing and fixating forces, fail to acknowledge men (sic!) as historical beings; problem-posing theory and practice take man's (sic!) historicity as their starting-point."[103]

Inasmuch as it recognizes that human beings are beings in the process of becoming, are unfinished, never completed realities (so is sub-human reality, but it does not know this), problem-posing education, too, must be "constantly remade in the praxis"[104]: this kind of education must become in order to be; it lives in a kind of dialectic tension between permanence and change. It accepts "neither a 'well-behaved' present nor a pre-determined future (and) roots itself in the dynamic present and becomes revolutionary".

103 *Pedagogy*, p. 56.

104 *Ibid.*, p. 57.

As "revolutionary futurity" it is prophetic and hope-filled and thus corresponds to the historical nature of the human person:

> ... it affirms men (sic!) as beings who transcend themselves, who move forward and look ahead, for whom immobility represents a fatal threat, for whom looking at the past must only be a means of understanding more clearly what and who they are so that they can more wisely build the future. Hence, it identifies with the movement which engages men (!) as beings aware of their incompleteness, a historical movement which has its point of departure, its subjects and its objectives.[105]

Whereas the banking System sees the people's situation as fatalistic, investing it with a naive, mystico-mythico-magical quality, the dialogical system enables the oppressed to recognize their situation as limiting and oppressive, but not fated and unalterable. This provokes a "movement of inquiry" towards their set-up and provokes them to engage with others in order to achieve authentic and full humanization which is our historical vocation. Such a movement cannot be attained in isolation and individualism: it can only be realized in solidarity and fellowship. Any attempt to prevent anyone, on whatever grounds, from engaging in this form of critical enquiry is tantamount to violence, for it forcibly reduces human to the level of objects. Furthermore it violates the humanity of both those who are prevented as well as of those who do the preventing.

> No one can be authentically human while he prevents others from being so. The attempt to be more human, individualistically, leads to having more, egotistically. Not that it is not fundamental to have in order to be human. Precisely because it is necessary, some men's (!) having must not be allowed to constitute an obstacle to others' having, to consolidate the power of the former to crush the latter.[106]

105 *Pedagogy*, p. 57.

106 *Pedagogy*, p. 58.

Problem-posing education, as humanist and liberating praxis, "posits as fundamental that men (!) subjected to domination must fight for their emancipation". Hence, it seeks to render both students and teachers as subjects of the educational process, overcoming both authoritarianism and an alienating intellectualism. Nor can the banking method be used, even as an interim measure, to be replaced later by the genuinely 'revolutionary approach. Revolutionary education must be revolutionary, that is, dialogical, right from the very outset!

Dialogue and "Naming"

Dialogue, as a human phenomenon, is derived from action (work) and reflection (word): this is authentic praxis. For word without action is mere verbalization, alienated and alienating 'blah'! And action without reflection is activism, action for action's sake, without any proper goal or motive.

> Human existence cannot be silent, nor can it be nourished by false words, but only by true words, with which men (!) transform the world, to change it. Once named, the world in its turn reappears to the namers and requires of them a new naming. Men (!)are not built in silence, but in word, in work, in action-reflection.[107]

Praxis is not inimical to "the silence of profound meditation", that authentic retreat whereby we only apparently leave the world we withdraw from, only in order to consider it more fully, in its totality-thus, in effect, ever remaining with it, ever 'bathed in it'! An inauthentic retreat is a kind of "historical schizophrenia', as it implies cutting oneself off from the world, through contempt and fear, a flight from the world. Besides, this "naming" of the world must not be taken as "the privilege of some few men (!), but the right of every man (!)."[108] For "no one can say a true word alone-nor can he (!) say it for another, in a prescriptive act which robs others of their words", since true dialogue is "the encounter between men (!), mediated by

107 *Pedagogy*, pp. 60-61.

108 *Ibid.*. p. 61.

the world, in order to name the world": it cannot occur between those who want to name the world by themselves and those who do not want to accept this meaning. Before the act of authentic naming of the world can take place, those who've been denied their right to do so must "reclaim this right and prevent the continuation of this dehumanizing aggression."[109]

Qualities Presupposed by Authentic Dialogue

a) Love: Inasmuch as dialogue implies the act of re-creating our broken world it is impossible if not infused with a "profound love for the world and of men (!)." Here Freire quotes, with approval, those powerful words of Che Gruevera, "The true revolutionary is guided by strong feelings of love. It is impossible to think of the true revolutionary without this quality."[110] He continues,

> No matter where the oppressed are found, the act of love is commitment to their cause-the cause of liberation. And this commitment, because it is loving, is dialogical. As an act of bravery, love cannot be sentimental; as an act of freedom, it must not serve as a pretext for manipulation. It must generate other acts of freedom; otherwise, it is not love. Only by abolishing the situation of oppression it is possible to restore the love which the situation made impossible. If I do not love the world-if I do no love life-if I do not love men (!)-I cannot enter into dialogue.[111]

b) Humility: This is another concomitant of authentic dialogue. For if we wishto name the world, in collaborative solidarity with the oppressed, this cannot take place as long as one elite group sees itsel alone as persons and views the rest as a collection of 'its', clubbing them together with disparaging titles as "the masses" or "the great unwashed". Humility is truth and involves recognizing that the participants in dialogue are neither a bunch of utter ignoramuses nor

---

109 *Pedagogy*, p. 61

110 *Pedagogy*, p. 62.

111 *Ibid.*

a college of perfect sages, but a group of human "attempting together to learn more than they now know".

c) Faith: Furthermore, dialogue calls for "intense faith" in human beings, in their ineluctable capacity to re-create. It is grounded on the conviction that no amount of oppression can utterly efface in the human heart a desire to grow more fully human, more fully alive. The true "dialogical person" believes in others, even before concretely meeting them. Nor is this a naive faith, but a critical one. One is fully aware that our inherent ability to create and transform can be-and often is-impaired by a profoundly alienating situation. One's conviction is that, at most, this dehumanizing situation can only harm this capacity, never utterly destroy it. And one sees such a situation as a challenge, not a cause for despair. One remains convinced that this power, however apparently dead, can be restored, not gratuitously, but by a struggle for liberation.

d) Trust: This cannot but result from the interaction of the above three qualities. How could a loving, humble and faith-filled dialogue not bring about a climate of mutual trust, drawing all together in the great task of emancipation. Faith in people is the pre-condition for dialogue and trust is the natural consequence of it, for trust can only arise when one sees by another's actions that this others words and intentions are sincere.

> To say one thing and do another-to take one's own word lightly-cannot inspire trust. To glorify democracy and to silence people is a farce; to discourse on humanism and to negate man (!) is a lie.[112]

e) Hope: This is another pre-condition for dialogue. It is "rooted in men's (i) incompleteness, from which they move out in constant search ... in communication with others", whereas hopelessness is "a form of silence, of denying the world and fleeing from it". The dehumanization resulting from an unjust, oppressive situation should lead, not to despair, but to hope. Nor is hope a matter of folding one's hands and passively waiting for a deliverer, but a going forth in pursuit of the humanity injustice has denied.

112 *Pedagogy*, p. 64

> As long as I fight, I am moved by hope and, if I fight with hope, then I can wait. As the encounter of men (!) seeking to become more fully human, dialogue cannot be carried on in a climate of hopelessness. If the participants expect nothing of their struggle, their encounter will be empty and sterile, bureaucratic and tedious![113]

f) Critical Thinking: This is radically different from naive thinking and is an absolute requirement for authentic dialogue. It involves recognizing that there is an indivisible bond that binds human to their world; furthermore it perceives reality as a dynamic thing, ever in the process of transformation, rather than something static and finished; finally it is a form of thinking that naturally flows into risk-taking action. Naive thinking is just the opposite and so is a block to genuine dialogue for, in effect, it sees historical time as a dead weight, something unchangeable, laden with the experiences of the past: hence all must one do is adapt oneself to it-any attempt to critique, much less change it, is seen as a subversion of order. Critical thinking, on the other hand, seeks to further the meaningful transformation of reality so as to assure the continued transformation of the human person.

Dialogue vs Anti-Dialogue

If problem-posing education is dialogical, the banking system of education is anti-dialogical, inasmuch as it perpetuates the false dichotomy of teacher (active) and student (passive).

> ... the dialogical character of education as the practice of freedom does not begin when the teacher-student meets the student-teachers in a pedagogical situation, but rather when the former first asks himself (!) what his dialogue will be about. And preoccupation with the content of dialogue is really preoccupation with the programme content of education.[114]

---

113 *Pedagogy*, p. 65.

114 *Ibid.*

In anti-dialogical education, the educator answers his own question, without consulting the students or taking them into account. The educator organizes his own programme and sets his own topic and themes. Thus, the programme-content in anti-dialogical education consists of bits of information to be deposited, or foisted upon, hapless students. In dialogical education, the students help determine the programme-content. It is a matter of teaching the people "clearly what we have received from them confusedly", as Mao puts it in his Anti-memoirs. The former approach involves the teacher bringing to the students the various projects or programmes that he/she think they need. In dialogical education, one sets about to discover the felt needs and problems of the people: after all the fundamental objective of the revolutionary leader-teacher-student is

> ... to fight alongside the people for the recovery of their stolen humanity, not to "win the people over" to (one's own)side. Such a phrase does not belong to the vocabulary of revolutionary leaders, but to that of the oppressor. The revolutionary's role is to liberate, and be liberated with the people-not to win them over.[115]

Thus, whereas in the anti-dialogical approach, it is carried on by A for B or by A about B, the methodology of dialogical educations involves carrying it out by A with B, mediated by the world which impresses and challenges both parties, provoking their reactions and exchange.

The students, too, are viewed differently by both ways. The anti-dialogical approach ignores the concrete, existential situation of the people and seeks to lodge a "deposit" in them. The dialogical method recognizes that they are persons-in-a-situation and, hence, their situation has to be taken seriously, as part of their subjecthood.

Finally both ways differ as to their goals, also. The former focuses on the people as objects to be indoctrinated so that they learn to adjust to an inviolate, unchangeable reality; the latter trains its attention on the reality that has to be transformed.

---

115 *Pedagogy*, p. 67.

In short, the banking approach encourages passivity in the oppressed: it takes advantage of their "submerged" consciousness to augment their fear of freedom (hence, no changes!).' In authentic dialogue, the educator is not so much preoccupied with providing an "alternative filling" to the consciousness of the oppressed, but rather making them aware of' the fact that they have somehow internalized or "housed" the oppressor who must be "ousted" before the authentic action for liberation can begin. Well-meaning but misled revolutionaries see themselves as Messiah-figures who have to go to the people in order to bring them a message of salvation. The authentic leader seeks, through dialogue, to discover the people's objective situation and help them to penetrate layers of false "mythicisation" to come to an awareness of it. Then, through action reflection-action he/she works with them towards deeper liberalization and humanization.

Generative Themes

Animals, unlike humans, can't distance themselves from their situation or actions and critically reflect on these. They have no in-depth awareness comparable to humans. Any "decision" they make is more a "species decision" than a personal choice. By that same token, they can't take real risks for they are unable to realize all the attendant circumstances and consequences of a risk. They live in a kind of overwhelming present, in which the world is but a remote back-drop that accompanies them, without assuming the proportions of any real challenge or task.

But humans, on the other hand, are deeply aware of themselves, their activity and their world. We act in function of objectives proposed, evaluated and chosen by our own personal decisions. We infuse the world with our creative presence and can radically transform it for good or for ill. We are historical beings: space and time are real for us. We can perceive that certain configurations constitute veritable "limit situations" for us, i.e. they limit or put restrictions to our fuller human development. Now these "limit-situations" can be either helplessly perceived as impassable boundaries which curtail our possible development, or as challenging frontiers that separate us from fuller humanness, from being yet more-as boundaries to be fought against and overcome. Experience shows us, furthermore, that as soon as one limit-situation is overcome, another looms threateningly on the horizon.

A little reflection will enable us to recognize that there are certain "generative themes" which "both contain, and are contained by, limit situations". These are called "generative" themes because they have within them the capacity to generate other themes, which might call for yet other tasks to be fulfilled. Thus, a slum may become aware of the limit situation of not having clean water (or electricity) as being a severe block to the health (or development) of the people. But this, after reflection, might be found to be inseparably linked with their helpless dependence on the whims and fancies of corrupt land-lords or municipal officials. As they move from recognition of effects and their causes, symptoms and the malady bringing them about, they are putting their finger on ... "generative themes" Part of the problem, at this point, is dialoguing with the people so as to bring them to an awareness that their situation is not something immutable, "fated" and inevitable: it is something artificial, contrived, created by vested interests, who want it to be maintained at all costs. Most of all, the people must become convinced that something can be done about it and, ultimately, it is they who must initiate the action for justice. But this action must be accompanied as well as preceded by critical reflection and planning: no haphazard "launching into the deep" will assure them the realization of their goals.

> Consequently, liberating actions in a historical milieu must correspond not only to the generative themes but to the way in which these themes are perceived. This requirement implies another: the investigation of meaningful thematics.[116]

Generative themes are best elaborated in concentric circles, going from the more general to the more particular (or vice versa). Arguably the most fundamental theme of our epoch is domination: its objective would be the opposite them, liberation. Breaking this down into more particular themes, we come across underdevelopment, linked to dependency, linked to colonial legacies and so on.

---

116 *Pedagogy*, p. 75.

Coding and De-Coding

The concrete oppressive situation consists of a complex of interactive elements that come together and support each other. Bow it is imperative that the people see them not as constituting a paralysingly vast, impenetrable whole which envelops everyone and everything in some irresistible manner. This would call for a moment of analytic reflection, of "coding", i.e. exploring the existential situation so as to high-light its constituent interacting elements. Correspondingly, there will also be a need for "decoding", in other words, a critical analysis of the coded situation:

> Its 'decoding' requires moving from the abstract to the concrete; this requires moving from the part to the whole and then returning to the parts; this in turn requires that the Subject recognize himself (!) in the object (the coded concrete existential situation) and recognize the object as a situation in which he finds himself, together with other Subjects."[117]

Thus, through decoding, the people begin to exteriorize their view of the world and how they see it: fatalistically, dynamically or socially (in other words, they're spelling out thereby their "generative themes"). If a group is totally unable to express its generative theme, this suggests not so much the non-existence or absence of such a theme, but "a very dramatic theme: the theme of silence": "The theme of silence expresses a structure of muteness in the face of the overwhelming force of the limit-situations."[118]

It stands to reason, of course, that the "investigation of themes involves the investigation of the people's thinking."[119] It is no question of one or some men thinking out all this for the others: however superstitious or naive the people may initially be, it is ultimately they who must be taught to think for themselves, however difficult or time-consuming this may be. The people have borne centuries of

117 *Pedagogy*, p. 77.

118 *Ibid.*, p. 76.

119 *Ibid.*, p. 80.

misery: it is better that they bear it a little longer and learn to change their own false notions out of conviction. “Producing and acting upon their own ideas-not absorbing those of others-must constitute that process.[120] And they must be led to do this for themselves by way of an “objective-problematic” whereby they are brought to awareness of their true situation by being confronted with it such that they no longer see it as a “dense, enveloping reality or a tormenting blind alley” from where there is no exit.

> Men (!) emerge from their submersion and acquire the ability to intervene in reality as it is unveiled. Intervention in reality-historical awareness itself-thus represents a step forward from emergence and results from the conscientisation of the situation. Conscientisation is the deepening of the attitude of awareness characteristic of all emergence.[121]
>
> Thus, thematic investigation deepens historical awareness and is thereby educational; conversely, all authentic education provokes re-thinking. Unlike the banking approach, the dialogical method is constituted by the way the students view their world and it is thence that they elaborate their own generative themes. This invariably involves the dialogical “teacher” working with an inter-disciplinary team (which includes certain key personalities from among the people) to “re-present” the peoples’ view”.

In a first, exploratory stage investigators (among whose number, let it be once again emphasized, must be numbered significant representatives of the people) note how the people tend to view their world. This will involve a critical analysis (or splitting up) of “the enormous, unique, living ‘code’” that has to be “deciphered”. By breaking it up into its constituents, the people are helped to see how these elements inter-act, inter-penetrate and thus create and sustain each other. This is done by being present at key moments in the life of the people (their celebrations, the way they express themselves in

120 *Pedagogy*, p. 80.

121 *Ibid.*, p. 81.

work, play, prayer) and in casual conversations (in casual husband-wife or parent-child exchanges, in meetings with peers, officials and elders. All this is necessary to "decode" the "code" by collecting a wealth of apparently insignificant detail: without this, no real decoding is possible.

Then comes the crucial second stage. Here all listen in to how each person, in his or her decoding attempt, has perceived the various events and situations. Everyone reacts, shares and critiques the others' comments. It goes without saying that the people's output and input are of crucial worth, here. Inevitably, at least some of the participants will be led to re-consider their previous comments and, in this way, the situation is unveiled. This way of resolving "contradictions" is more efficacious in leading up to plans of action more likely to succeed than one that is "imposed from on top"! This would throw "real consciousness" into bold relief, as against "potential consciousness".

> Real consciousness is the result of the multiple obstacles and deviations that the different factors of empirical reality put into opposition and submit for realization by the potential consciousness.[122]

Now the above terminology has been borrowed by Freire from Goldmann. This "real consciousness", Freire points out, is, at first, unable to perceive the "untested feasibility" that lies beyond the limit situation. After all, "real" or "recent" consciousness tends to see the set-up as pre-ordained, given, something to be passively accepted. It does not yet recognize that an overthrow of the unhappy and unjust situation is feasible-that possibility remains "untested" and so the fact that it is "potential" is not even considered. Where Goldmann spoke of "potential consciousness", Freire preferred "un-tested feasibility": this is similar to Nikolai's "unperceived practical solutions". Once these have been unveiled it is not too difficult to figure out how to proceed.

122 *Pedagogy*, p. 85.

Some Common Erroneous Procedures

The most vicious of these is based on a lack of faith in the peoples' capacity to liberate themselves and their oppressors from the curse of dehumanization. This mixed in with a yearning for 'quick results' has led many a sincere revolutionary to 'launch a revolution for the benefit of the ignorant masses'. They're too brain-washed to recognize what is their own good, is the claim. Thence, the revolutionary tries, at first, to coax and cajole the people into following his directives. Then, as he loses patience with their slow response, he becomes yet another oppressor of the masses, terrorizing them and punishing them for not letting him liberate them! It was Lenin who had rightly said, "without a revolutionary theory, there can be no revolutionary movement". Now the only relevant revolutionary theory here is the one that recognizes that the people must be party to their own revolution and must be admitted into both levels of the necessary praxis, action and reflection. Leaders can, at most, co-ordinate and, sometimes even, direct the movement, but if they deny the people a role in praxis and usurp it for themselves alone, they are invalidating it by that same count! For the above reasons, a military coup cannot amount to an authentic revolution for it is based on deceit, rather than on dialogue. True revolution can only be legitimized by dialogue with the people.

> It cannot fear the people, their expression, their affective participation in power. It must be accountable to them, must speak frankly to them of its achievements, its mistakes, its miscalculations and its difficulties.[123]

The earlier the dialogue begins, the more truly revolutionary will the movement be. As soon as one hinders dialogue or impedes people's participation, one would be reducing them to the status of mere things ... and thus one would be doing the oppressors' job! Nor does genuine praxis allow a splitting up of reflection and action: first pure reflection and then pure action: both must be carried out concomitantly. However, critical reflection may decide that certain

---

123 *Pedagogy*, pp. 98-99.

forms of action are inadvisable for the moment. This is permissible as it has been preceded by critical reflection which is itself a form of action.

> The revolution is made neither by the leaders for the people, nor by the people for the leaders, but by both acting together in unshakeable solidarity. This solidarity is born only when the leaders witness to it by their humble, loving and courageous encounter with the people. Not all men (!) have sufficient courage for this encounter-but when men (!) avoid encounter they become inflexible and treat others as, ere objects; instead of nurturing life they kill life; instead of searching for life, they flee from it. And these are oppressor characteristic.[124]

Another destructive approachis to reject the conviction that dialogue alone can transform the people and their world as "naively and subjectively idealistic."[125] But, in reality, there is nothing more real, concrete and dynamic than "men (!) in the world and with the world, than men (!) with other men (!)-and some men (!) against others, as oppressing and oppressed." Authentic revolution seeks to remedy this dehumanizing state of affairs-nor can we expect those who're profiteering from the set-up to be the one's to initiate the change! Only the tyrannized, with their leaders, can do this. This, in turn, presupposes that the leaders have incarnated the people's perspective through authentic communion with them. In consequence, the people's previously fatalistic and mechanistic view of the world gets transformed and their false consciousness gets corrected.

> There is no historical reality which is not human. There-is no history without men (!), and in history for men (!) there is only history of men, made by men and (as Marx pointed out, in turn making them). It is when the majority are denied their right to participate in history as Subjects that they become dominated and alienated. Thus, to supersede

124 *Pedagogy*, p. 100.

125 *Ibid.*

> their condition as objects by their status of Subjects-the objective of any true revolution-requires the people to act, as well as reflect, upon the reality to be transformed.[126]

What would be really idealistic and naive is to imagine that humans could become full Subjects merely by reflection, without action: by becoming aware of their oppressive situation. At most, this would make them, in the telling phrase of the Honduran activist, Fernando Garcia, "Subjects in expectancy". Equally unreal would be to hold that mere activism (unaccompanied by reflection) would be the road to revolution. And, it should be emphasized, it must be the people, not the so-called "revolutionary leaders" acting in isolation from them that must be the agents of this action-reflection praxis. It is only the dominant Elites and the pseudo "leaders of the people" who come from them that don't want the oppressed to think for them-selves. Freire quotes the kind of spurious arguments mouthed by such persons who do their utmost to make it sound that resisting the education and conscientisation of "the masses" would only be to their own good. Thus the justification proceeds:

> However specious in theory might be the project of giving education to the labouring classes of the poor, it would be prejudicial to their morals and happiness; it would teach them to despise their lot in life, instead of making them good servants in agriculture and other laborious employments; instead of teaching them subordination it would render them fractious and refractory, as was evident in the manufacturing countries; it would enable them to read seditious pamphlets, vicious books and publications against Christianity; it would render them insolent and in a few years the legislature would find it necessary to direct the strong arm of power against them. (Quoting a certain Mr. Giddy, "later President of the Royal Society", *Pedagogy*, p. 102)

The Absolutisation of Ignorance is a key oppressor myth and is the mainstay of much resistance to authentic liberation activity.

126 *Pedagogy*, p. 101.

It alleges that "the masses" are imbued with this quality ineluctably as their birth right: they are conceived in ignorance, live in it and must die in that state. It is bad enough when the oppressor believes it, arrogating to himself the sole right to use words, name things and make judgments (even judgments about what the oppressed's "real problems" are and how they should be resolved). What is even more lamentable is the fact that not a few would-be liberators of the people subscribe to this calumny. Under the guise of "saving time", they substitute slogans for dialogue and foist upon a hapless and reluctant people a diagnosis and a treatment for all their ills.' But no one can, strictly speaking, "set another free": at best we can create conditions that will facilitate the other's attainment of self-freedom,

> A free action can only be one in which a man changes his world and himself. ... A positive condition of freedom is the knowledge of the limits of necessity, the awareness of human creative possibilities.... The struggle for a free society is not a struggle for a free society unless through it an even greater degree of individual freedom is created.[127]

The Characteristics of Antidialogical Action

These particularly characterize repressive regimes and it is not too surprising that pseudo-revolutionaries seek and find inspiration from these attitudes. After all, such leaders are more interested in seizing, wielding and maintaining power than in liberating the people: indeed, the view the latter as a mere means to fulfil their primary goal!

a) Conquest: The antidialogical person employs a wide spectrum of approaches under this rubric, from the most solicitous paternalism to the most ruthless repression. This consists, basically, in imposing his objectives on the vanquished, housing himself in them. Now, just as dialogue is concomitant with every phase and step of liberation, so antidialogue becomes indispensable to the preservation of the situation of conquest. This is invariably aided and abetted by "myth-making" and by dint of continual repetition, the oppressed people

---

127 *Pedagogy*, p. 107, a quote from Gajo Petrovic.

come to accept these myths as Gospel truths and denounce all those who question them as "enemies of freedom". Among such myths we may list the following (the list is not exhaustive): the myth that the oppressive set-up is actually a "free" society, the myth that all workers are always free to choose their jobs and can seek alternative employment (and find it!) if they don't agree with their boss, the myth that the social set-up respects human rights and is worthy of esteem, the myth that the worker and the boss are really equal in every way, the myth that the "charity" and false generosity of the elites is totally disinterested, the myth that rebelliousness is a sin against God's will, the myth of the industriousness and superiority of the oppressors and of the laziness and "barbarity of the oppressed, the myth the oppressor is bravely defending religious and moral values against godless materialism ...

b) Divide and Rule: This is a technique of keeping people repressed and submerged that is as old as oppression itself. For the oppressive minority just cannot afford to let the oppressed majority unite and organize themselves for a struggle for liberation.

> It is in the interest of the oppressor to weaken the oppressed still further, to isolate them, to create and deepen rifts among them. This is done by varied means, from the repressive methods of governmental bureaucracy to the forms of cultural action with which they manipulate the people by giving them the impression that they are being helped.[128]

One of the most subtle ways of doing this is to champion a "focalized" approach to the peoples, talking of "problems", but with a particularly pernicious slant. After all, such an approach is also employed in the dialogical method, but with a radically different orientation: in the latter the local community or its problems as seen as part of a totality and linked to the whole, whereas in the former the stress is on the individual group or issue, which is viewed in such a way as to ignore the wider context. Thus we have the red herring of "leadership courses" which, in the long run, alienate the leaders from the people. Potential leaders are selected, withdrawn

128 *Pedagogy*, p. 111.

from the community, trained in isolation, within the context of a totally different life-style and then "sent back" as betters to their inferiors, whose respect they have by then lost and who no longer can fit in with the people's way of speaking, living and interacting. In a dialogical approach, the entire community is trained to lead. In the process either the former leaders of the people are confirmed or they're replaced by new Emergent one's.

c) Manipulation: This subtle procedure becomes necessary as soon as the people begin to notice their oppression and start getting restive. As long as they were totally "submerged" there was no need to manipulate them. As soon as the first warning signs of conscientisation and restiveness are detected and before this gets transformed into dangerous aggressivity, it becomes imperative to distract them from all this by giving them the impression that certain concessions have been granted them-this is what is meant by manipulation. ....

Now it is the urban proletariat that is more susceptible to manipulation: inasmuch as they are found in the more industrial centres, consider themselves relatively privileged and rather large in number. So the powers that be make a great show of "granting them their organizations" and initiating a "pseudo-dialogue", the main purpose of which is to ensure that the people don't think. Populist leaders are given the center of the stage, are petted and pampered, made to feel that they are a great success as they are photographed and headlined as they shuttle back and forth between the Elites and the people they are supposed to represent. Authentic dialogue with the people directly is branded as time-consuming, bourgeois and reactionary. Instead their intermediaries are lionized, befriended and ... manipulated. It is difficult to manipulate all the people (you can't fool all of the people all of the time). But you can manipulate their "representatives"-especially if you play a subtle role in deciding just who these will be.

d) Cultural Invasion: This approach involves the oppressors invading the cultural context" of the oppressed, ignoring and pushing it aside and, finally, imposing their own world view in its place. Slowly the message gets across that "to be cultured" means to abandon one's native mores, feel ashamed of it and assume the lifestyle of the oppressors, walking, dressing, talking, singing and dancing like their invaders.

> Whether urbane or harsh, cultural invasions thus always an act of violence against the persons of the invaded culture, who lose their originality or face the threat -of losing it. In cultural invasion (as in all the modalities of antidialogical action), the invaders are the authors of, and actors in, the process; those they invade are the objects. The invaders mould; those they invade are moulded. The invaders choose; those they invade fallow that choice-or are expected to follow it. The invaders act; those they invade have only the illusion of acting through the action of the invaders.[129]

Now the results of this cultural invasion are deep-rooted and destructive-even emasculating, one could say. For it leads to making the invaded feel that they are "culturally inauthentic", that the only way they can become "cultured" is to mimic the cultural values, standards and goals of their invaders: once again, we have the cultural "I" of the invaded (oppressed) person housing the personality of the invader and the duality of the underdog is back with a vengeance.

The Emergence of Authentic Revolutionary Leadership

Invariably, such leaders come from the ranks of former dominators. They are men and women whose existential experience has opened their eyes to the oppressive situation of which they were a part and has led them to seek true solidarity with the oppressed. This would imply sentiments of true commitment and love within them. However, they must make themselves ware of certain "oppressor attitudes" that they still enshrine within their personalities and get rid of them, such as the conviction that they alone know what is best for the people, their tendency to view things from the perspective of the false myths they themselves have propagated, and so on. Thus, the *characteristics of dialogical action* slowly begin to assert themselves:

a) Co-operation: This is marked contrast to the dominating "teacher" making a conquest of the "masses, transforming the

---

129 *Pedagogy*, pp. 121f.

vanquished into mere "things". In this approach, the student-teacher and the teacher-students meet in cooperation to transform the world. This does not mean that there is no role for revolutionary leadership in dialogical action; rather, it means that the leaders, however important and crucial their role may be (and is!) derive no right thereby to hustle the people blindly towards their "salvation"!

> Such a salvation would be a mere gift from the leaders to the people-a breaking of the dialogical bond between them, and in a reduction of the people from being co-authors of liberating action into the objects of that action.[130]

Such co-operation can only be achieved through authentic communication and dialogue and dialogue doesn't manipulate, domesticate or "sloganize". Again, this doesn't mean that the one who dialogues has no goals or objectives; rather is committed to the objective and goal of freedom. Now, it is a contradiction in terms to try and 'conquer the people for freedom: this is but seeking the adhesion of the vanquished to the conqueror's wishes. Just as the antidialogical approach seeks the mythicisation of the world (so as to maintain the status quo), the dialogical approach seeks to unveil it (so as to transform it). Nor can one unveil the world for another: such an action must be done by full-fledged Subjects for themselves!

b) Organization: Just as manipulation was a key element in the antidialogical-approach, organization becomes indispensable for dialogical leaders: this is how they build unity, a unity between the people and their leaders as well as among the people themselves. This calls for "constant, humble and courageous witness" of leaders and people for the common task of liberation. More concretely, this would entail consistency between words and actions, a boldness which does shrink from taking up more or less permanent risks in the struggle for freedom, radicalization of thought leading to committed action (hence, a far cry from mere 'sectarianism'), faith In the people who are the ultimate Subjects of their own liberation (this implies a sincere and profound love for them and their humanization). The support

130 *Pedagogy*, p. 136.

of the people may be slow and hesitant in coming, but unless and until it comes there can be no true revolutionary action for justice.

> Since witness is not an abstract gesture, but an action-a confrontation with the world and with men (!)-It is not static. It is a dynamic element which becomes a part of the societal context in which it occurred; from that moment, it does not cease to affect that context.[131]

c) Unity for Liberation: Now this is the very antithesis of the dominators' 'divide and rule policy'. This is no easy task, also because the dialogical leaders cannot use any of the 'short-cut' methods that the dominators don't scruple to employ, nor have they power on their side. The oppressor aims, at most, to secure some short-term unification of the people, more or less obliging them to join in the fight against the "common" adversary (the revolutionary leader who is-actually the enemy of only the oppressor)! Since the oppressors are unconcerned about the feelings and opinions of the people, "unity" for them means a mere unity among themselves-something which they can attain quite easily. The revolutionary leader, however, has to seek the more difficult path of communion with the oppressed, combating their inherent "oppressor-oppressed" dualism, integrating their cognitive, affective and active dimensions as full Subjects.

> The objective of dialogical-liberative action is not to 'dislodgel the oppressed from a mythological reality in order to 'bind' them to another reality. On the contrary, the object of dialogical action is to make it possible for the oppressed, by perceiving their adhesion, to opt to transform an unjust reality.[132]

d) Cultural Synthesis: Oppressive or liberative action cannot but have a bearing on existing social structures, which imply certain cultural values. Domination seeks to suffocate and uproot the socio-cultural values of the people, as incarnate in their various structures

131 *Pedagogy*, p. 144.

132 *Pedagogy*, p. 141.

and replace them with those of the oppressors, transplanted into the soil of the oppressed. In liberative action, one seeks to preserve the people's culture, inasmuch as this promotes and enhances the full flowering of each and every person, irrespective of sex or any other consideration. As and when the people begin to recognize that certain aspects of their structural set-ups do not bring this about, they themselves seek to remove them.

Antidialogical cultural action seeks, to eradicate the people's culture and replace it with that of the oppressors and, by employing myths (such as that of "God's will"), aims to render permanent and inviolable the transplanted one. They go to the people indirectly (through technology and the mass media), superimposing themselves on the latter, reducing the people to the level of passive spectators, static 'things' who have to be transformed to the advantage of their "betters"! Dialogical action involves going to the people directly, building real communion with them and thereby aiming, along with them, to elicit liberative action that would human singly transform their world.

> Those who are invaded, whatever their level, rarely go beyond the models which the invaders prescribe for them. In cultural synthesis, there are no invaders; hence, there are no imposed models. In their stead, there are actors who critically analyses reality (never separating this analysis from action) and intervene as Subjects in the historical process.[133]

Only in cultural synthesis is the opposition between the world-view of the people and that of their leaders resolved-to the enrichment of both.

And the only way to this is by meeting, dialogue and mutual challenge.

> In the antidialogical theory of action, cultural invasion serves the end of manipulation, which in turn serves the ends of conquest, and conquest serves the ends of domination.

---

133 *Pedagogy*, p. 148.

> Cultural synthesis serves the ends of organization; organization serves the ends of liberation.[134]

Conclusion

Now that the wheel has gone full circle, illumined by Freire's telling analysis of revolution, we can cry out, in mock paraphrase of Madam Roland as she mounted the steps to the guillotine during those heady days of the French Revolution (and which can be found on the opening pages of this text, "O Revolutionaries and Liberators, what crimes are committed in your name!"

Freire's compelling words throw light on why so many terrorist organizations, from the Taliban to Boko Haram or ISIS end up only adding more suffering and oppression to the people they claim to liberate and sometimes, with the best of intentions, do but substitute one group of feelingless and merciless dominators with another, while the condition of the oppressed remains the same ... if not gets progressively worse!

Some Quotes

"There was reason to fear that, like Saturn, the Revolution might devour each of its children in turn."

– Pierre Vergniaud

"When a wave of love takes over a human being... such an exaltation takes him that he knows he has put his finger on the pulse of the great secret and the great answer."

– Marjorie Kinnan Rawlings

"Real education enhances the dignity of a human being and increases his or her self-respect. If only the real sense of education could be realized by each individual and carried forward in every field of human activity, the world will be so much a better place to live in."

– A. P. J. Abdul Kalam

134 *Pedagogy*, p. 150.

BIBLIOGRAPHY

Aggestam, Karin, and Annika Björkdahl. 2013. *Rethinking Peacebuilding: The Quest for Just Peace in the Middle East and the Western Balkans, Routledge Studies in Peace and Conflict Resolution*. London; New York: Routledge.

Aquinas, Thomas. 2012. *Summa Theologiae Prima Pars, 1-49, The Complete Works of Saint Aquinas*. Lander, WY: Aquinas Institute for the Study of Sacred Doctrine and Aquinas, Thomas. 2012. *Summa Theologiae Prima Pars, 50-119, 14*. Lander, WY: Aquinas Institute for the Study of Sacred Doctrine.

Aseh, Nfamewih. 2006. *Political Philosophies and Nation-Building in Cameroon: Grounds for the Second National Liberation Struggle*. Buea, Cameroon: Global Vision for Development Alternatives.

Berger, Peter L. 1979. *The Heretical Imperative: Contemporary Possibilities of Religious Affirmation*. 1st ed. Garden City, N.Y.: Anchor Press.

Bernier, Normand R., and Jack E. Williams. 1973. *Education for Liberation: Readings from an Ideological Perspective*. Englewood Cliffs, N.J.: Prentice-Hall.

Berofsky, Bernard. 1995. *Liberation from Self: A Theory of Personal Autonomy*. Cambridge; New York: Cambridge University Press.

Birch, Charles, and John B. Cobb. 1990. *The Liberation of Life: From the Cell to the Community*. Denton, Tex.: Environmental Ethics Books.

Boff, Leonardo. 1985. *Church, Charism and Power: Liberation Theology and the Institutional Church*. New York: Crossroad.

Cardenal, Ernesto. 1976. *Gospel in Solentiname,* New York: Orbis Books.

Cassano, Graham, and Richard Alan Dello Buono. 2010. *Crisis, Politics and Critical Sociology, Studies in Critical Social Sciences*. Leiden; Boston: Brill.

Catholic Church. *Catechism of the Catholic Church.* Liguori, MO: Liguori P.

Ciprut, Jose V. 2008. *Freedom: Reassessments and Rephrasings*. Cambridge, Mass.: MIT Press.

Culclasure, Scott P. 1999. *The Past as Liberation from History, Counterpoints*. New York: P. Lang.

Dalton, Dennis. 1996. *Freedom the Philosophy of Liberation*. Springfield, VA: The Teaching Company (sound recording).

Daly, Mary. 1973. *Beyond God the Father: Toward a Philosophy of Women's Liberation*. Boston: Beacon Press.

De Villiers, Pieter. 1987. *Liberation Theology and the Bible, Miscellanea Congregalia*. Pretoria: University of South Africa.

Desbruslais, Cyril. 1985. *The Philosophy of God*. Pune: Jnana Deepa Vidyapeeth, (mimeographed notes).

Desbruslais, Cyril. 1989. *Interpretations of Transcendence*. Pune: Jnana-Deepa Vidyapeeth.

Dussel, Enrique D., and Eduardo Mendieta. 1996. *The Underside of Modernity: Apel, Ricoeur, Rorty, Taylor, and the Philosophy of Liberation*. Atlantic Highlands, N.J.: Humanities Press.

Dussel, Enrique D., and Eduardo Mendieta. 2003. *Beyond Philosophy: Ethics, History, Marxism, and Liberation Theology, New Critical Theory*. Lanham, Md.: Rowman & Littlefield Publishers.

Dussel, Enrique. 1985. *Philosophy of Liberation*, trsl. Martinez and Markowsky, New York: Orbis Books.

Fanon, Frantz, and Richard Philcox. 2004. *The Wretched of the Earth*. New York: Grove Press.

Freire, Paulo, and Antonio Faundez. 1989. *Learning to Question: A Pedagogy of Liberation*. New York: Continuum.

Freire, Paulo. 1972. *Pedagogy of the Oppressed,* trsl. Myra Ramos, Penguins, Hammondsworth.

Fromm, Erich. 2010. *The Heart of Man: Its Genius for Good and Evil.* Riverdale, New York: American Mental Health Foundation Books.

Garaudy, Roger. 1967. *From Anathema to Dialogue: The Challenge of Marxist-Christian Cooperation*. London: Collins.

Gibbs, Benjamin. 1976. *Freedom and Liberation, Philosophy Now*. New York: St. Martin's Press.

Giri, Ananta Kumar. *Knowledge and Human Liberation: Towards Planetary Realizations*. London: Anthem Press.

Gould, Carol C., and Marx W. Wartofsky. 1976. *Women and Philosophy: Toward a Theory of Liberation, Capricorn Books*. New York: Putnam.

Grob, Leonard, Riffat Hassan, and Hayim Gordon. 1991. *Women's and Men's Liberation: Testimonies of Spirit, Contributions in Philosophy*. New York: Greenwood Press.

Gutiérrez, Gustavo, Marc H. Ellis, and Otto Maduro. 1989. *The Future of Liberation Theology: Essays in Honor of Gustavo Gutiérrez*. Maryknoll, N.Y.: Orbis Books.

Gutiérrez, Gustavo. 1988. *A Theology of Liberation: History, Politics, and Salvation*. Maryknoll, New York: Orbis Books.

Harris, Sharon M., and Linda K. Hughes. 2013. *A Feminist Reader: Feminist Thought from Sappho to Satrapi*. 4 vols. Cambridge, UK; New York: Cambidge University Press.

Harrison, Faye Venetia, and Association of Black Anthropologists. 1997. *Decolonizing Anthropology: Moving Further toward an Anthropology of Liberation*. 2nd ed. Arlington, Va.: Association of Black Anthropologists, American Anthropological Association.

Hawkins Benedix, Beth. 2009. *Subverting Scriptures: Critical Reflections on the Use of the Bible*. 1st ed. New York: Palgrave Macmillan.

Heraclitus, and T. M. Robinson. 1987. *Fragments, Phoenix Supplementary Volume*. Toronto; Buffalo: University of Toronto Press.

Hoger Katechetisch Instituut (Nijmegen Netherlands). 1969. *A New Catechism; Catholic Faith for Adults, with Supplement*. New York: Herder and Herder.

Huxley, Aldous. 1946. *The Perennial Philosophy*. London: Chatto and Windus.

Jaspers, Karl. 1948. *Der Philosophische Glaube*. Zürich: Artemis Verlag..

Jaspers, Karl. 1968. *The Perennial Scope of Philosophy*. Hamden, Conn.: Archon Books.

John Paul II, Pope. 1988. *Encyclical Letter Sollicitudo Rei Socialis of the Supreme Pontiff, John Paul II, to the Bishops, Priests, Religious Families, Sons and Daughters of the Church and All People of Good Will for the Twentieth Anniversary of Populorum Progressio*. Washington, D.C.: Office of Publishing and Promotion Services, United States Catholic Conference, 1988.

Leahy, Michael P. T. and Dan Cohn-Sherbok. 1996. *The Liberation Debate: Rights at Issue*. London; New York: Routledge.

Lewin, Kurt. 1951. *Field Theory in Social Science; Selected Theoretical Papers*. 1st ed. New York: Harper Lewis, Oscar. 1961. *The Children of the Son*. New York, Random House.

Loyola, Ignatius, and George E. Ganss. 1991. *Ignatius of Loyola: The Spiritual Exercises and Selected Works, The Classics of Western Spirituality*. New York: Paulist Press, no. 325.

Marcel, Gabriel. 1952. *Metaphysical Journal*. London: Rockliff.

Marcel, Gabriel. 1949. *Positions concretes du mystere onto-logiaue*. Paris: Vrin.

Maréchal, Joseph. 1944. *Le point de départ de la métaphysique: leçons sur le développement historique et théorique du problème de la connaissance*. Bruxelles; Paris: L'Édition universelle; Desclée, De Brouwer.

Marsh, James L., and Anna J. Brown. 2012. *Faith, Resistance, and the Future: Daniel Berrigan's Challenge to Catholic Social Thought.* 1st ed. New York: Fordham University Press.

Marshall, Donald G. 2005. *The Force of Tradition: Response and Resistance in Literature, Religion, and Cultural Studies.* Lanham: Rowman & Littlefield.

McLaren, Peter, and Colin Lankshear. 1994. *Politics of Liberation: Paths from Freire.* London; New York: Routledge.

Micklem, Nathaniel. 1941. *The Theology of Politics.* London, New York etc.: Oxford University Press.

Moltmann, Jürgen. 1993. *Theology of Hope: On the Ground and the Implications of a Christian Eschatology.* 1st Fortress Press ed. Minneapolis: Fortress Press.

Monden, Louis. 1966. *Sin, Liberty and Law.* London: Dublin, G. Chapman.

Mootz, Francis J. and George H. Taylor. 2011. *Gadamer and Ricoeur: Critical Horizons for Contemporary Hermeneutics, Continuum Studies in Continental Philosophy.* London; New York: Continuum.

Moses, Greg and Jeffrey R. Paris. 2006. *Liberation between Selves, Sexualities, and War, Radical Philosophy Today.* Charlottesville, Va.: Philosophy Documentation Center.

Nuccetelli, Susana; Ofelia Schutte, and Otávio Bueno. 2010. *A Companion to Latin American Philosophy, Blackwell Companions to Philosophy.* Malden, MA: Wiley-Blackwell.

Oosterlaken, Ilse and Jeroen van den Hoven. 2012. *The Capability Approach, Technology and Design, Philosophy of Engineering and Technology,.* Dordrecht; New York: Springer.

Pandikattu, Kuruvilla. 1999. *Idols to Die, Symbols to Live: Dynamic Interaction between Language, Reality and the Divine.* Intercultural Pub, New Delhi.

Pieris, Aloysius. 1988. *Love Meets Wisdom: A Christian Experience of Buddhism, Faith Meets Faith.* Maryknoll, N.Y.: Orbis Books.

Posner. R. 1992. *Sex and Reason,* Cambridge (US): Harvard University Press.

Powell, David, Tom Hickey, and Colin Richmond. 2007. *Democracy: The Long Revolution*. London; New York: Continuum.

Rahner, Karl. 1968. *Sacramentum Mundi: An Encyclopedia of Theology*. 6 vols. London: Burns & Oates. Vol. IV.

Russell, Bertrand. 1927. *An Outline of Philosophy.* London: Allen and Unwin.

Sartre, Jean-Paul. 1938. *La nausea*. Paris, Gallimard.

Sartre, Jean-Paul. 1967. *Bariona*. 2e édition Paris: E. Marescot.

Shea, William M. 2004. *The Lion and the Lamb Evangelicals and Catholics in America*. Oxford; New York: Oxford University Press. http://site.ebrary.com/id/10103522.

Silva, Ignacio Alberto. *Latin American Perspectives on Science and Religion*, *International Perspectives on Science, Culture and Society*. London: Routledge.

Stern, J. P. 1979. *Nietzsche*. Glasgow, Fontana/Collins.

Taliaferro, Charles, and Paul J. Griffiths. 2003. *Philosophy of Religion: An Anthology*, *Blackwell Philosophy Anthologies*. Malden, MA: Blackwell Pub.

Wittgenstein, Ludwig. 1992. *Tractatus Logico-Philosophicus*, *International Library of Psychology, Philosophy, and Scientific Method.* London; New York: Routledge & K. Paul.

GLOSSARY OF SELECT TERMS

Albigensianism: Members of a Catharistic sect of southern France flourishing primarily in the 12th and 13th centuries. Exterminated in the 13th century by a crusade led by Pope Innocent III.

Anawim: A Hebrew word that means, "the poor who depend on the Lord for deliverance."

Androgogics; from andragogy: The method and practice of teaching adult learners; adult education.

Anḗr: From Greek (genitive); m, third declension. man (**adult** male) husband.

Biophily: Love for life or humans subconsciously seeking connection with the rest of life.

Catharism; from the Greek: καθαροί, katharoi, "the pure ones". It was a Christian dualist movement that thrived in some areas of Southern Europe. Catharism was a Christian dualist movement that thrived in some areas of Southern Europe, particularly northern Italy and southern France, between the 12th and 14th centuries. Cathar beliefs varied between communities because Catharism was initially taught by ascetic priests who had set few guidelines. The Catholic Church denounced it.

Decalogue: The Ten Commandments of the Bible.

Docetism: The doctrine, important in Gnosticism, that Christ's body was not human but either a phantasm or of real but celestial substance, and that therefore his sufferings were only apparent.

Doxa: A Greek word meaning common belief or popular opinion, from which are derived the modern terms of orthodoxy and heterodoxy.

Hermeneutical circle: The hermeneutic circle (German: *Hermeneutischer Zirkel*) describes the process of understanding a text hermeneutically. It refers to the idea that one's understanding of the text as a whole is established by reference to the individual parts and one's understanding of each individual part by reference to the whole.

Ideology: A (narrow?) system of ideas and ideals, especially one which forms the basis of economic or political theory and policy. In contrast to *Weltanschuung*, ideology tends to be more rigid and fixed.

Manicheism: A dualistic religious system with Christian, Gnostic, and pagan elements, founded in Persia in the 3rd century by Manes or Mani (c. 216–c. 276) and based on a supposed primeval conflict between light and darkness. It was widespread in the Roman Empire and in Asia, and survived in eastern Turkestan until the 13th century.

Masters of Suspicion: The French philosopher Paul Ricoeur famously coined the phrase 'the masters of suspicion' to describe Marx, Nietzsche and Freud. In fact, they are all dependent on their predecessor Ludwig Feuerbach and challenges us to question religion thoroughly and reach at a purified faith.

Mauvaise foi: "Being of bad faith" or "insincere" or "dishonest" or "not genuine" or "not straight up".

Mystery: Unlike a problem, mystery is a situation where I am deeply involved and so which can never be solved. It can be encountered and its meaning may be grasped ever more. Gabriel Marcel understands being as simply "that which resists exhaustive analysis." Examples of mystery for Marcel are love, friendship, life and death.

Necrophily: Abnormal attraction, especially erotic, to corpses, implying sometimes sexual intercourse with or attraction towards corpses. In general, it is love of death.

Panentheism: Belief that everything is in God, unlike pantheism, which holds that everything is God.

Pedagogics or pedagogy: the method and practice of teaching, especially as an academic subject or theoretical concept.

Perennial philosophy: The *Perennial philosophy* (Latin: *Philosophia Perennis*), is a perspective in the *philosophy* of religion which views each of the world's religious traditions as sharing a single, universal truth on which foundation all religious knowledge and doctrine has grown.

Picture theory of language: The picture theory of language, also known as the picture theory ofmeaning, is a theory of linguistic reference and meaning articulated by Ludwig Wittgenstein in the *Tractatus Logico-Philosophicus*. Wittgenstein suggested that a meaningful proposition pictured a state of affairs or atomic fact.

Religionless Christianity: Influenced by modernism Dietrich Bonhoeffer, German theologian who was killed by Nazis, saw a time coming in which religion would prove to be fundamentally irrelevant. "We are moving towards a completely religionless time; people as they are now simply cannot be religious anymore. Even those who honestly describe themselves as 'religious' do not in the least act up to it, and so they presumably mean something quite different by 'religious'..." He adds: "And if therefore man becomes radically religionless—and I think that is already more or less the case (else, how is it, for example, that this war, in contrast to all previous ones, is not calling forth any 'religious' reaction?)—what does that mean for 'Christianity'?"

Sein des Seienden: This Heideggerian phrase denotes the "Being of beings." The first Being is used in the verbal sense and the latter as entities or individual beings. So the phrase denotes the coming to be of beings.

Weltanschauung: German for world-view, perspective or larger vision of reality. Used in a broad and general sense. So it is one's overall-comprehensive philosophical vision.

Weltoffenheit: Openness to the world, a term introduced by German theologian Wolfhart Pannenberg.